Hitting Low in the Zone

A NEW BASEBALL PARADIGM

HOMER BUSH
WITH MONICA GREER

paige 1 PUBLISHING

TULSA, OK // NASHVILLE, TN

98 W.S. Champs

Hitting Low in the Zone: A New Baseball Paradigm
Copyright ©2015 by Homer Bush. All Rights Reserved.

No part of this publication may be reproduced, stored in a retrieval system or transmitted in any way, by any means, electronic, mechanical, photocopy, recording or otherwise without prior permission of the author except as provided by USA copyright law.

Published by Paige1Publishing
Tulsa, OK | Nashville, TN
918.706.4359 | www.paige1publishing.com

Paige1Publishing works with authors on a variety of projects, providing resources and tools neccessary to replicate excellence in the publishing industry.

Sports teams, businesses and trademarks mentioned in the book are not the property of the author and are used solely for educational purposes.

Published in the United States of America
ISBN: 978-1-937250-77-5
1. Sports: Baseball;
2. Sports: Baseball Instruction;

"I hold it that a little rebellion now and then is a good thing, and as necessary in the political world as storms in the physical."
—**Thomas Jefferson**

"Baseball people are generally allergic to new ideas. It took years to persuade them to put numbers on uniforms, and it is the hardest thing in the world to get Major League Baseball to change anything — even spikes on a new pair of shoes — but they will eventually . . . they are bound to."
—**Branch Rickey**

"Think for yourself along rational lines. Hypothesize, test against the evidence, never accept that a question has been answered as well as it ever will be. Don't believe a thing is true just because some famous baseball player says that it is true."

—**Bill James**

Homer

*To my team Monica, Jailyn and Homer Jr.
and my mom, Charlene*

Monica

*To my support system Alisha, Kirk, Nanishka and my mom,
Deanna and my Bombers teammates*

Acknowledgements

Throughout this book, I have attempted to cite and give credit to all sources and authorities used; any omission is purely accidental. Many of the statistics and charts relied on were found at **brooksbaseball.net.** *Brooks Baseball* was an unbelievable resource for me, and I thank them for helping me sort the data and for providing specialized queries.

Being blessed with athletic ability, I focused on sports as a way out of the inner city. Growing up among hundreds of talented kids with the same goal, the odds were against me. But at each critical stage of my life, through sports, there were surrogate parents, influential and positive people to take care of and guide me in the right direction. To all of them I say, "Thank you from the bottom of my heart."

Marlon Dozier (brother and 1st unofficial baseball coach); Reverend Dr. William and Martha Gillespie; Larry and Diane Neal (1st youth baseball coach); Bob Shannon (high school football coach); Arthur May (high school baseball coach); Richard and Russell Krause (RJ Krause All-Stars); Van Smith (San Diego Padres scout); and later Priscilla Oppenheimer (San Diego Padres); Cito Gaston (former hitting coach, Toronto Blue Jays); and Joe Torre (former manager, New York Yankees).

I would also like to thank my family for all of their support over the life of my baseball career: Maxie Dozier, Charletta Dozier, Marian Dozier, Annie Bush, Clark Bush and James Bush.

Table of Contents

FOREWORD 11

PART I: A Player's Perspective 17
    Chapter 1 19
    My Journey

PART II: Let's Get Down to Hitting 23
    Chapter 2 25
    The Majority of Pitches Are Thrown Low in the Zone
    Chapter 3 35
    The Best Hitters are Successful in the Lowest Part of the Hitting Zone
    Chapter 4 49
    A Universal Approach to Hitting: Preparation, Focus and Execution

PART III: Swing Mechanics 57
    Chapter 5 59
    The Game Plan
    Chapter 6 65
    The Grip and Stance
    Chapter 7 67
    The Load
    Chapter 8 69
    The Swing Path
    Chapter 9 77
    The Shift

PART IV: The Team Approach 79
    Chapter 10 81
    Teams Need Consistent Run Production to Make the Postseason
    Chapter 11 85
    How Hitting Low in the Zone Affects Payroll
    Chapter 12 89
    Do Teams Put Too Much Emphasis on Walks?
    Chapter 13 95
    How Statistics Can Make or Break a Team
    Chapter 14 101
    Conclusion

My Afterthoughts and Hope for the Future of Baseball 103

Foreword

At one time, people thought the Earth was the center of the universe and were convinced it was flat. To say otherwise was heresy. In 1776, a group of colonists thought a government of the people, by the people and for the people was preferable to a monarchy. Their radical ideas were considered treason to the King of England. Nearly 250 years later, the United States is the most powerful nation on Earth (which, by the way, is round and revolves around the sun), and our Constitution has withstood the test of time.

Why were these ideas opposed and rejected at first? Because they challenged long-held beliefs and, if true, would alter the balance of power. For over 150 years, baseball has loyally adhered to the notion that a pitch properly executed, thrown low in the hitting zone cannot be consistently hit into play with success. In other words, if a pitcher makes his pitch, the batter has virtually no chance to get on base. Even in 2014, Rick Kranitz, pitching coach for the Milwaukee Brewers, was quoted as saying, *"That's really where we teach all our pitchers to pitch [low in the zone]. If the ball gets in the air, there are a heck of a lot more places the ball can be an extra-base hit or a home run."* [1]

Without risk of the same consequences that faced our founding fathers (at least I hope), I write this book to help coaches and hitters understand that the aforementioned age-old notion is flawed, and hitters can find significant success against pitches thrown in the lowest part of the hitting zone—even if the pitcher "makes his pitch." In the process, two major benefits occur. First, hitters will be able to see a material increase in their batting averages and overall production numbers. Second, teams can score runs more efficiently and in greater volume that will allow them to accumulate what matters most: wins.

---

[1] David Leonhardt, "Small Change Looms Large: The Strike-Zone Revolution," The New York Times (Oct. 23, 2014)

Hitting Low in the Zone: A New Baseball Paradigm

With a proper understanding of the "hitting zone" and swing path, backed up by empirical evidence on pitch location, hitters will be more likely to get a hit from a pitch thrown low in the hitting zone than they would with a pitch thrown in the upper part of the hitting zone. Through supporting data, photographic analysis and plain old common sense, this book will help readers realize: (1) the greatest opportunities for hitters exist in the lowest part of the hitting zone, which is where the majority of pitches are thrown; (2) the hitters with the **highest** batting averages **are** successful in the lowest part of the hitting zone; (3) it is the batter's swing path – not the pitcher's pitch – that determines the trajectory and direction of the ball off the bat; and (4) the proper hitting mechanics (combined with discipline) will allow hitters to consistently drive low pitches for success. If this process is adopted as a team approach to hitting so that it is repeated at-bat after at-bat, runs may be scored more efficiently and in greater volume.

Why is this radical? First, my philosophy challenges the notion that good pitching always defeats good hitting. Second, I believe batters can be successful if they slightly alter their vision of what is a hittable pitch. Success can be achieved by swinging at pitches low in the hitting zone that are not clearly strikes from a rule book definition of the strike zone but are nonetheless very hittable. Third, I advocate for a team approach to hitting whereby the collective good is paramount and less emphasis is placed on individual statistics.

How do we know there are lots of pitches to hit low in the zone? Pitchers are groomed from the first day they take the mound in Little League all the way through to the big leagues, to pound the lower part of the zone so they can induce ground balls. How often have you heard analysts fault a pitcher for allowing his pitch to drift up in the strike zone after a big hit occurs? In most cases, advanced level pitchers intentionally throw a pitch "up" in the zone in order to: (a) get hitters to swing and miss; (b) create weak fly balls; or (c) set up the next pitch (usually low and away). So why should hitters take the bait? They shouldn't. They should focus on the lower part of the zone – the place where the pitcher wants to throw the ball. Then when a pitcher throws low in the zone, the number of times a batter will swing and miss or fail to put the ball in play successfully will go down significantly. In turn, the balance of power may dramatically shift.

With the approach discussed in this book (*looking low in the zone and applying the correct swing path*), it is easy to see that players should improve in areas such as:

(1) the number of pitches they see; (2) their ability to hit more line drives; (3) establishment of better counts to hit in; and (4) accessibility to more and better contact. As a result, a hitter's statistics should improve in average, on-base-percentage, slugging percentage, on-base plus slugging percentage, hits, runs batted in, walks and extra-base hits. By extension, and with a consistent approach, teams will improve too.

The teams that collectively have the highest batting averages against pitches thrown 2 ½ feet and below in the hitting zone and average scoring more runs than they allow are the teams that are most likely to reach the postseason. The difference between teams that make or miss the playoffs is, on average, approximately one offensive run per game. That's it—just one single run. And the teams that score more runs do so because they have more hits in the same number of games. Thus, teams that want to reach the postseason need more hits in order to reach the postseason. Shouldn't teams look for those hits where most pitches are thrown?

Let me be clear about one thing. Despite the use of data in this book, it is not about Sabermetrics or a challenge in any way to it. Teams are now staffed with economists and statisticians that crunch data and look at algorithms to find trends that can help them build better teams in the hope of winning more games, and they add immense value to the game. This book is not written for them. I don't even speak their language. This book is written for the guy that stands inside the chalk box. It is a book written by a player, for the player, to help him improve his day-to-day performance. We live in a world that craves new information and reinvention and values looking at things from different perspectives. Indeed, doing so should lead to more reliable facts and inevitably lead to improvement.

As I tested the approach described in this book with others, there were many who refused to consider an idea that challenged conventional wisdom because it was contrary to long-held personal beliefs. I found it startling that those whose job it was to make teams and players better wouldn't seriously consider the idea that I had come up with something new – or at least something important that had been overlooked. They would refute the notion with their belief that most pitches aren't low in the zone and hitters can't be successful with them.

At first, I thought it was just me. Maybe it was how I was delivering my message? Maybe I was just plain wrong? But like many who believe deeply in an idea,

I refused to accept rejection. I dug in deeper and continued to test my theories, studied the game, the great hitters of today and the past and spoke to highly credentialed former ball players. At the end of that process, I was more convinced than ever that what I have pieced together—and is the crux of this book—is a highly potent hitting philosophy that should make virtually all hitters much better and teams much more competitive.

However, I was still puzzled by the certainty of those who had rejected the concepts in this book. Then I read a book by John Sexton, the President of New York University (and serious baseball fanatic), called *Baseball as a Road to God: Seeing Beyond the Game.* In that book he discusses the conflict that arises when facts get in the way of faith and used baseball as a backdrop. He describes his driver, Tippy, who was a walking encyclopedia of baseball statistics and facts. On a few occasions, Tippy provided Sexton with "feats that (according to Tippy) had been accomplished only once in the entire history of the game." Examples of these "facts:"

> **Question 1:** Who is the only player in baseball history to have hit an inside-the-park grand slam home run?"
> **Answer 1:** Mel Stottlemyre.
>
> **Question 2:** Who is the only player in baseball history to hit a home run in his first major league at-bat and a triple in his second and then never hit a home run or triple thereafter?
> **Answer 2:** Hoyt Wilhelm.

Sexton thought the answers were plausible for a number of reasons and eventually re-posed these questions to hundreds of people, including former Secretary of State Henry Kissinger. One evening, however, his facts were challenged. Using the information superhighway, his friend looked up the answer to Question 1 on the spot and determined that Sexton (and Tippy) was dead wrong. Based on his friend's quick search, he discovered forty players (including the great Roberto Clemente) had accomplished that feat since 1950 alone!

Sexton's initial reaction was to "deny the evidence" and affirm his belief. When confronted, Tippy reacted in the same way. But Sexton was no longer certain of the "facts" and began to challenge all that Tippy had told him. He then discovered that Tippy was wrong about Hoyt Wilhelm too. Wilhelm had in fact hit a home run in his first at-bat, but the triple did not occur until the following season. However, they were the only home run and triple of his career. Sexton reflected on these events with the following:

> *Tippy's tale reveals the perils of hubris and certitude, unleavened by doubt. And it displays the ways those who claim the Truth with a capital T—religious or otherwise, from popes to drivers—react when science (the advancement of what we know) throws into question the basis of belief. Tippy simply would not let the facts get in the way.*[2]

This story helped me to understand why some would reject an idea they long-held to be true. There are some who are willing to seek the truth and will then reshape their beliefs along rational lines. And there are those who, with nothing to lose and everything to gain, will not budge from their beliefs in the face of facts. I realized I cannot change those people. I can only accept who they are (because they are otherwise good people) and not let it shake my confidence. Therefore, in the pages that follow, I will lay out the factual basis for my theory and provide actual examples of it in today's game.

It is often said that "youth is wasted on the young." As I get older and more knowledgeable about my craft, I believe that phrase to be 100% true. If I knew at 22 what I know today, I would have significantly extended my career. I would want to know—mechanically—why I was having success so I could repeat it time and time again. But at this point, I simply hope to make a difference in the lives of anyone who knows what it feels like to hold a baseball bat in their hands and stare at a figure on a bump sixty feet, six inches away and feel like the pitcher has the edge. When most hitters come to bat, they are looking for a pitch in a specific location. Every now and then they'll look for a certain type of pitch, but typically it's location that matters. This book will demonstrate that most pitches are thrown low and once we know their location, it's time to get to hacking. After reading this book, I hope you will understand that **you** always have the edge at the plate and your improved individual statistical performance and team record will be the proof. In time, perhaps, pitchers will be forced to adjust how they approach hitters when they realize that the lowest part of the hitting zone is not a safe haven. And then we will need to—yet again—challenge what becomes the conventional wisdom of how to beat it.

---

[2] Sexton, John, "*Baseball as a Road to God: Seeing Beyond the Game*" (2013) pp 68-72.

Part I

A Player's Perspective

Chapter 1

MY JOURNEY

We are all products of where we come from and I am no different. My aggressive style on the bases, making the most of the opportunities presented to me, and above all my willingness to be a team player all have their roots in how I grew up. The approach to hitting and team-oriented strategy I advocate in this book (and even the way I tested my assertions) are all reflections of the life I have lived. I try to make the most of every opportunity, maintain intense focus, be part of a larger team effort and surround myself with good people who will provide sound advice and help keep me on the right path. This formula has worked for me as someone who came from a place where very few would bet that I would someday make it to the major leagues and be part of a world championship team that would rewrite record books.

I did not play organized baseball until I was 12 years old. In retrospect, that was probably a good thing. I was always athletic, so I let my God-given ability carry me, and I did not get inundated with too much mechanical information. I was introduced to baseball by my older brother, Marlon "Doe" Dozier, and he was, effectively, my first coach. He would keep things simple by saying, "*Head, just see it, then put the fat part of the barrel on the ball.*" By keeping things simple, I was able to be aggressive, have fun and figure out things for myself. Today, youth baseball is totally different. Parents hire coaches to give their kids batting lessons at 6 years old and pitching lessons at 8 years old. Kids are working on their mechanics before their bodies even begin developing. And the information they are being given may not be correct: "get your back elbow up," "swing down on the baseball," "swing level to the baseball" and "widen your stance." So, not only do kids lose the opportunity to play in a fun and stress-free environment (it is, after all, just a game), they also miss out on the best way to learn the game: through trial and error. Players want to be perfect out of the box, when in reality making mistakes (especially in practice) is an important way to learn things.

Once I started playing organized baseball, I was good enough for my coaches to just let me play and they didn't change a whole lot with my game. Like Doe had told me, I kept it simple. All I thought about was being aggressive, playing hard, putting the ball in play and using my speed. But I learned that if I swung at a high fastball, I was probably going to swing and miss or strike out. I know that approach is nothing special, but at least I had figured out that much on my own—and not because someone simply told me not to swing at high pitches. In high school I started to hit for more power. I don't know how or why the power came, but it did, and my approach remained the same. In one game during my high school senior season, I hit two home runs, each estimated to have traveled over 400 feet. After that game I always wondered why I could not hit home runs more often because I clearly had enough power to do it. At the time, I attributed it to luck—largely because that was what my coach told me, and then he advised that I go back to focusing on hitting ground balls due to my speed. I now know that it wasn't luck. The reason that I know that it wasn't luck is because through my research I've found that every hitter has to elevate the ball the same way. A home run is just a by-product of getting the ball into the air. And in order to get the ball into the air over and over again, a hitter needs to repeat the same proper swing path and mechanics, which I will discuss further in Part III of this book.

After my senior year in high school, I was picked by the San Diego Padres in the seventh round of the amateur draft. Once I got into pro ball, hitting coaches would tell me to swing down on the ball to get backspin. They would say "a little guy like you needs to focus on line drives and hitting the ball up the middle and the other way." As an 18-year-old kid, this sounded good, but I still needed to learn some basics: How to hold the bat properly, what my stance should look like and how I should swing the bat in order to get the results my coaches wanted. Needless to say, I was confused and didn't know what to do. Unfortunately, it showed. I struggled in the first couple games. Then, I went back to what I knew best: Get low in my stance, lay off the high fastball and put the ball in play. Largely using my own technique, I finished my rookie season with a .323 batting average. The next year when I reported to spring training, the Padres asked me to try to cut down on my strikeouts, increase my walks **and** hit .300+ again. They didn't say **how** to do any of this; they just wanted it done. So, in order for me to accomplish what the team wanted, I felt like I had to wait until the pitcher got two strikes on me before I could think about swinging. I'm sure this sounds familiar to a lot of hitters today with so much emphasis having been put on on-base percentage (OBP). As you can imagine I found myself behind in the count and chasing pitches late in my at-bats. As a result, my average suffered, my strikeouts when up and my walks did not increase. The experiment was a failure. Once I got home to East St. Louis, I realized that the best chance I had to make the major leagues was to rely on the skills that got me drafted. I went back to basics again: I got low in my stance, I got more aggressive and when I got a pitch I could handle, I put the fat part of the barrel on the ball. Once I went back to *my way* of doing things, my career began to take off. Speaking of *"my way,"* that style clearly caught the attention of the New York Yankees, who traded for me and Hideki Irabu in 1997.

The biggest test of my career came in the spring of 1998. Whatever I knew about hitting had to be displayed during the first thirty days of spring training because I was out of options and the Yankees had no roster spots available. The most likely outcome would be to play well enough to be traded. I had to consider that they had just traded for Chuck Knoblauch, a three-time All-Star second baseman. If I didn't I would be sent down to the minors and probably never be heard from again. I remember driving back to my apartment thinking that I had come too far to fail so my only option was to play well. I went to the field each and every day looking to "zone down" and lay off the high fastball. I did just that and found myself on the opening day roster for the New York Yankees. I can't describe how easy hitting came to me with this simple approach. That year, I even won an award for being the best rookie of the spring training. Previously, I had no idea that the award even existed and was truly honored and surprised. I would later learn that the Yankees had been awarding this since 1956 and the past recipients make a truly impressive list: Tony Kubek, Johnny Blanchard, Tom Tresh, Roy White, Willie Randolph, Don Mattingly, Al Leiter, Hensley Muelens, Gerald Williams and Jorge Posada. Since 1988, the award has been given to other worthy individuals including Alfonso Soriano, Nick Johnson, Hideki Matsui and Brett Gardner.

Hitting Low in the Zone: A New Baseball Paradigm

Being a member of the 1998 world championship team did so much for me and my career. I'm pretty sure most people think that I'm talking about the World Series ring itself and the additional monetary bonus that comes from winning the World Series. Those things were awesome, but being around all the veteran and superstar players each and every day is what I remember most. Being a role player, I had the chance to either talk hitting or watch hitters who are considered to be some of the best to ever play the game. I took full advantage of this opportunity because I thought it unlikely that it would ever happen again. I watched and studied Derek Jeter's famous inside out swing, Chuck Knoblauch's and Bernie Williams' low batting stances, Paul O'Neill's famous over exaggerated head down practice swing, Darryl Strawberry's uppercut swing, Tim Raines' Walt Hriniak style swing and Chili Davis' sweet swing from both sides of the plate. I also received some of the most invaluable instruction one could ever imagine from Yankee legends such as Reggie Jackson, Mickey Rivers, Willie Randolph and Chris Chambliss. I ended up hitting .380 in 1998 playing in a limited role from opening day to the end of the season, and I credit that to being immersed in conversations about and witnessing some of the best hitting in baseball and then being able to take what I'd learned and execute it throughout the season. A good friend of mine, and avid baseball guy, did a search and found that if you take a subset of players from 1923 to 2007, with between 78 and 99 plate appearances in a single season, I ranked 10th in batting average overall.[3] This is a pretty big deal knowing how difficul it is to be successful when you're not getting consistent at-bats.

Different approaches and mechanics generate various types of success which is evident in the players mentioned earlier. Through data and analysis, you will learn that a large volume of a hitter's success is dependent upon where he looks for pitches. Through experience, I can attest that trying to look for a certain type of pitch each and every at-bat is extremely difficult. There are times when the hitter can look for a specific pitch and have some success but to maximize the likelihood of success, players should look for pitches by location and use the appropriate swing path.

---

3 http://www.baseball-reference.com

Part II

Let's Get Down To Hitting

Chapter 2

The Majority of Pitches Are Thrown Low in the Zone

The first component of my philosophy is not radical—maximize the hitter's opportunities to get base hits by looking at where most pitches are thrown. But before we do that, I'd like you to conduct a short visualization exercise. Imagine yourself standing at home plate with the perfect bat in your hands. The pitcher is not a person but a robot that can throw any pitch you want in any location that you want. What pitch would you tell the robot to throw you and in what location? My guess is that before you read this sentence, you had already answered: a four-seam fastball belt level or slightly higher over the middle of the plate. This is precisely the approach to hitting that I want to change and that I believe hitters are suffering from.

As you will see in the pages that follow, at most advanced levels of play, the belt-high fastball over the middle of the plate is, perhaps, **the least likely** pitch any hitter will see in an at-bat. So I ask the question, why would you consider that pitch the optimal one to swing at when there are the fewest number of opportunities to actually swing at it? Why would you spend most of your practice time on the pitches that you are least likely to see?

If you actually think about it for a few minutes, common sense will tell you that most pitches are thrown low in the zone. In fact, all evidence supports the notion that the overwhelming majority of pitches are thrown in the lower part of the hitting zone. Statisticians have spent a lot of time and effort confirming this fact. In October 2014, David Leonhardt wrote an article that appeared in The New York Times making the same observation and offering a potential cause:

> The strike zone is bigger than it used to be, especially around batters' knees. The change appears to stem from the league's growing use of video technology to evaluate umpires, which has led umpires to stick more closely to the official strike zone. And according to the rule book, the strike zone extends down to "the hollow beneath the kneecap." The enlarged strike zone, in turn, seems to be a major reason that strike-outs have risen and scoring has dropped sharply.
>
> Two different analyses of pitch-tracking software have found that the strike zone has grown almost 10 percent over the last five years. It grew in each of the last five seasons and more in 2014 than in any previous season. Five years ago, pitches just below 21 inches high and over the plate were rarely called strikes. This season, they usually were, according to one of the analyses, by Jon Roegele, which appeared in the publication Hardball Times.[4]

Even apart from the technical data, common sense also tells us that the low part of the strike zone is where hitters should focus. The vast majority of pitches thrown in the major leagues are four-seam fastballs, two-seam fastballs (a.k.a. a sinker), change-ups, curveballs and sliders. Of these five major types, four pitches (two-seam fastball, slider, curveball and change-up) are designed to break DOWN in (or out of) the strike zone. In fact, if thrown correctly, these pitches are made to look like strikes only to finish off the plate or below the strike zone. Only the four-seam fastball is intended to maintain a relatively flat trajectory, but gravity and other principles of physics naturally pull the ball down. So how often are these pitches thrown? Are four-seam fastballs most prevalent with a relatively flat trajectory up in the zone? The following chart shows the number of times the approximately 700,000 pitches were thrown in 2013 by pitch type.[5]

---

[4] David Leonhardt, "Small Change Looms Large: The Strike-Zone Revolution," The New York Times (Oct. 23, 2014)

[5] http://grantland.com/the-triangle/visualizing-patterns-in-mlb-pitching/.

Pitch	Amount Thrown	Percentage
Four-Seam Fastball	248,500	35.5%
Two-Seam Fastball	152,600	21.8%
Sliders	98,700	14.1%
Curveballs	69,300	9.9%
Changeups	66,500	9.5%
Other	64,400	9.2%
Total	700,000	100%

The first statistic that should jump out to the reader is that of all pitches the four-seam fastball is thrown only about 1/3 of the time. This does not take into account the left/left, left/right or right/right matchup. Nor does it take into account pitch location which—as we will see—does not tend to be belt high and middle of the plate. The second statistic that should stand out is that over 55% of all pitches thrown in 2013 were designed to break down in or out of the strike zone.

Four-Seam Fastballs

Four-seam fastballs are intended to have the flattest trajectories of all pitches, but nonetheless must have (as a matter of gravity and physics) some downward trajectory. A 6 foot 2 inch pitcher stands on a mound raised 10 inches off the ground and releases a ball from a location just above his head. A pitcher strides downhill taking some of the height off the point of release, but I think it can be safely said that the release point would be somewhere just above 6 feet. If the pitch remained on a flat trajectory for the 56 feet or so remaining between that point and the catcher's mitt, the ball would cross the plate over the batter's head for a ball. So the only way a four-seam fastball can make its way into the strike zone is if it has a downward trajectory from the pitcher's hand (i.e. release point). Four-seam fastballs, which represent 35% of all pitches thrown in 2013, finish in the middle or outside part of the plate and generally at the belt to mid-thigh (2 ½ to 3 feet from the ground).[6] Very few four-seam fast balls are in the upper part of the strike zone (i.e. at the letters or 4 to 4 ½ feet). The fewest number

---
6 Ibid

of four-seam fastballs are thrown above the hitter's belt. Therefore, if a hitter is looking for a four-seam fastball to hit, the most opportunities to get one will occur low in the zone.

Two-Seam Fastballs (or Sinkers)

Two-seam fastballs represented nearly 22% of all pitches thrown in 2013.[7] By its nickname (the "sinker") we already know the trajectory of this pitch. Sinkers are concentrated in the lower part of the strike zone. Two-seam fastballs don't usually finish in the up and away portions of the strike zone. But, the lower edge of the strike zone and below sees the highest concentration of sinkers.

Sliders

Sliders represented 14.1% of all pitches thrown in 2013.[8] The use of the slider increases or decreases depending upon the pitcher/batter matchup. Pitchers throwing to a batter standing in the box on the same side of his throwing arm (i.e. righty vs. righty or lefty vs. lefty) threw sliders 20% of the time. Conversely, pitchers throwing to batters standing in the box on the opposite side of his throwing arm (i.e. righty vs. lefty or lefty vs. righty) threw sliders only 10% of the time. Uniformly, however, virtually all sliders are thrown in the lower corners of the zone with the volume of pitches up and away almost non-existent. What is also important to note is that a high volume of sliders finish **low** and **outside** the strike zone.

Curveballs

Curveballs represented 9.9% of all pitches thrown in 2013.[9] While there are different types of curveballs (e.g. some break "12 to 6," others may have more lateral movement; some are thrown "off-speed"), the forward rotation of the baseball forces a downward trajectory. As a result, curveballs are uniformly in the lower 1/3 and corners of the hitting zone. Except for the occasional "hanging curveball," there are virtually no curveballs thrown in the upper most part of the

---
7 Ibid.
8 Ibid.
9 Ibid.

zone and very few will be in the middle of the zone.

Changeups

Changeups represented 9.5% of all pitches thrown in 2013.[10] Like the slider, the pitcher/batter matchup impacted the proportion of changeups thrown. Changeups were thrown more often in matchups where the batter is in the box opposite the pitcher's throwing arm. Changeups were thrown 17% of the time in lefty versus righty matchups and 12% of the time in righty versus lefty matchups. Similar to sliders and curveballs, changeups predominantly landed in the extreme lowest part of zone or below, and changeups in the higher part of the zone are virtually non-existent.

The chart below demonstrates the average drop of each pitch from a release point of approximately 6 ½ feet above the ground and 56 feet away from home plate. It also demonstrates that, on average, most pitches finished at approximately 2 ½ feet off the ground and below.

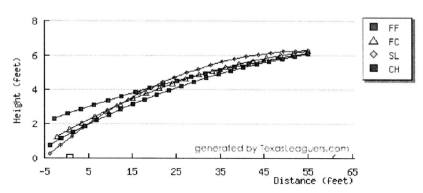

This chart confirms what common sense tells us: that most pitches—regardless of type—move on a downward trajectory from the release point into the strike zone. Let's look at the two Cy Young Award winners from 2013. Clayton Kershaw (lefty) is the 2011 and 2013 National League Cy Young Award winner. In 2013 he was 16-9 with an ERA of 1.83. In 2013, 61% of his pitches were fastballs (four and two-seam) and he threw a curve, slider or change-up for a combined 39% of the time. In fact, if you look at Kershaw's approach,

---

10 Ibid.

his "money pitches" are either the ones low in the zone or high and out of the strike zone to create a swing and miss.

One of the best websites for stats and details about each player in baseball is *brooksbaseball.net*. The following tables from Brooks Baseball shows the location of each one of Kershaw's pitches in 2013, first against right-handed batters and then against left-handed batters.

Clayton Kershaw: Raw Number of Pitches
From 01/01/2013 to 01/01/2014 | All Competition Levels
From the Catcher's POV: Against RHH
Against RHH

71 2.30%	107 3.47%	148 4.80%	89 2.89%	60 1.95%
94 3.05%	141 4.57%	133 4.32%	85 2.76%	68 2.21%
137 4.45%	181 5.87%	172 5.58%	127 4.12%	60 1.95%
151 4.90%	175 5.68%	147 4.77%	86 2.79%	76 2.47%
176 5.71%	218 7.07%	208 6.75%	112 3.63%	60 1.95%

Clayton Kershaw: Raw Number of Pitches
From 01/01/2013 to 01/01/2014 | All Competition Levels
From the Catcher's POV: Against LHH
Against LHH

20 2.24%	39 4.37%	37 4.15%	25 2.80%	12 1.35%
23 2.58%	51 5.72%	41 4.60%	27 3.03%	7 0.78%
52 5.83%	67 7.51%	56 6.28%	30 3.36%	10 1.12%
52 5.83%	50 5.61%	48 5.38%	21 2.35%	9 1.01%
61 6.84%	80 8.97%	46 5.16%	20 2.24%	8 0.90%

When viewed from this perspective, the data is even more compelling. Against right-handed or left-handed batters, Kershaw threw 45% of his pitches in the lowest 1/3 of the strike zone or below the strike zone.

Max Scherzer (righty) is the 2013 American League Cy Young Award winner with a record of 21-3 and an ERA of 2.90. In 2013, 56% of his pitches were fastballs (all four-seam) and he threw a curve, slider or change-up for a combined 44% of the time.

Hitting Low in the Zone: A New Baseball Paradigm

Max Scherzer: Raw Number of Pitches
From 01/01/2013 to 01/01/2014 | MLB Regular Season
From the Catcher's POV. Against RHH
Against RHH

12 0.91%	5 0.38%	15 1.13%	5 0.38%	2 0.15%
25 1.89%	31 2.34%	45 3.40%	34 2.57%	15 1.13%
28 2.11%	52 3.93%	80 6.04%	69 5.21%	59 4.46%
41 3.10%	58 4.38%	94 7.10%	99 7.48%	109 8.23%
25 1.89%	50 3.78%	76 5.74%	103 7.78%	192 14.50%

Max Scherzer: Raw Number of Pitches
From 01/01/2013 to 01/01/2014 | MLB Regular Season
From the Catcher's POV. Against LHH
Against LHH

70 3.43%	20 0.98%	13 0.64%	2 0.10%	1 0.05%
151 7.40%	56 2.74%	36 1.76%	15 0.73%	5 0.24%
222 10.88%	117 5.73%	112 5.49%	45 2.20%	20 0.98%
182 8.92%	133 6.52%	120 5.88%	71 3.48%	47 2.30%
127 6.22%	144 7.06%	157 7.69%	95 4.65%	80 3.92%

Both Kershaw and Scherzer threw pitches designed to break downward in (or out of) the strike zone between 40% and 44% of the time. In addition, some percentages of Kershaw's fastballs were two-seamed which more than likely brings them in line with the averages in the previous table. For those of you looking for that middle of the plate, belt-high four-seam fastball, both pitchers did that only 6-7% of the time in 2013 (and although I have not tracked when those pitches took place, I would offer an educated guess that a significant percentage occurred when the count was 3 and 0).

My own fact-finding is supported by a study by Jon Roegele that appeared in *The Hardball Times* on October 13, 2014. Roegele validated the prior work of academics Brian Mills and Jeff Sullivan that concluded that the strike zone has expanded when all called balls and strikes were examined year over year. Roegele also concluded that in 2014 the strike zone expanded almost entirely from strikes called in the bottom portion of the zone. Roegele stated, "*The average strike zone size increased by 16 square inches in 2014 over 2013, growing the zone to a robust 40 square inches larger than just five seasons prior. In the previous articles we discussed how the zone has actually been squeezing in at the sides slightly, but is stretching like crazy down from the knees as if it is under the clutches of gravity.*"

Roegele further found that "*the strike zone has had a full three inches—the diameter of a baseball—tacked onto the bottom within half a decade. . . . Previously I've shown that pitchers have been throwing to this expanding band at the bottom of the zone more and more each season to take advantage of the new pitcher-friendly area, and in turn hitters are now swinging more at pitches in this region. This is a trend that continued in 2014.*" Accordingly to Roegele, in 2014, 18.3% of all pitches thrown in 2014 were between 18" and 24" off the ground—49.2% of which are swung at. At the end of 2013, Roegele "calculated that the changing called strike zone had been responsible for about one third (31%) of the lower run environment in 2013 as compared to 2008." In 2014, "*yet again we see the number of expected runs decline, this time by 403 runs in a single year. As a frame of reference, if we subtract this number of runs from the league total in 2013, the average number of runs scored per team per game would have dropped from 4.17 to 4.08. Teams scored an average of 4.07 runs per game in 2014, the lowest total in not only the PITCHf/x era but since 1981.*" [11]

---

[11] Roegele, Jon, "*The Strike Zone Expansion is Out of Control*," The Hardballtimes.com, October 13, 2014, http://www.hardballtimes.com/the-strike-zone-expansion-is-out-of-control/

From this information, we can conclude that (a) most pitches are designed to break down, (b) pitchers (especially the elite) are throwing the majority of their pitches in the lowest parts of the strike zone and below and (c) umpires are, in fact, calling pitches strikes that are below the edge of the strike zone (from a rule book definition). These conclusions suggest that batters **must** learn to hit low pitches (those 18" to 24" off the ground) if they want to be successful and have a high batting average.

Chapter 3

The Best Hitters are Successful in the Lowest Part of the Hitting Zone

It is not accidental that I use the phrase "hitting zone" as opposed to the "strike zone" throughout this book. The two are not synonymous. The "strike zone" is defined in the rule book as *"that area over home plate the upper limit of which is a horizontal line at the midpoint between the top of the shoulders and the top of the uniform pants, and the lower level is a line at the hollow beneath the kneecap. The strike zone shall be determined from the batter's stance as the batter is prepared to swing at a pitched ball."*[12] As we know, the strike zone is subjective and will be interpreted according to the umpire calling balls and strikes at any particular game. Some days, the strike zone is high, low, wide or narrow. The "hitting zone" is a different concept: it is anywhere the batter is able to hit a baseball and make a proper, well executed swing resulting in solid contact. The hitting zone may well be below or outside what is considered a strike under the definition in the rule book.

All major league hitters swing at and make contact with balls out of the strike zone—some with more success than others. In 2013, Mike Trout of the Los Angeles Angels of Anaheim saw 3,033 pitches and batted .323 overall. Sixty-one percent (61%) of the pitches thrown to him were located **outside** the strike zone. Yet, Trout batted .283 when he swung at those pitches and put them into play.[13] Most hitters in baseball would gladly take an average of .283 for pitches **in** the strike zone, but Trout does it with the

---

12 Official Baseball Rules (2014 Ed.) Rule 2.00 at p. 21 (http://mlb.mlb.com/mlb/downloads/y2014/official_baseball_rules.pdf).
13 http://www.brooksbaseball.net/h_profile.php?player=545361&pFilt=FA|SI|FC|CU|SL|CS|KN|CH|FS|SB&time=month&minmax=ci&var=count&s_type=2&startDate=01/01/2013&endDate=12/31/2013&gFilt=regular

pitches that are intended to be balls or missed altogether. As we will see later, Trout is able to do so because his swing path gives him the ability to successfully hit low pitches (i.e. in the lowest part of the strike zone and below). The example of Mike Trout shows that by focusing on a **hitting zone** rather than a strike zone, the batter prevents the pitcher (or the umpire) from dictating what pitches he should swing at and in the process, makes the pitcher's job to locate unhittable pitches even more difficult. The key for a hitter is to control the hitting zone not the strike zone. Far too many hitters look for perfect strikes when what they should be looking for is the pitches that are the easiest to access and put the right swing on. Those pitches are down in the zone.

Empirical evidence and common sense have established that two-thirds of all pitches are thrown in the lowest part of the hitting zone. The next question is, are hitters successful in the lowest parts of the zone? The answer to that question will obviously depend upon the specific hitter. However, with the overall major league batting average in the low .250s, it is safe to assume that most are not proficient with pitches low in the zone.

Before we closely examine pitch location and results, let's first set up what we would expect to find. Again, common sense tells us that most hitters will pop up or hit fly balls on pitches up in the zone; hit line drives on pitches in the middle of the zone; and hit ground balls on pitches low in the zone. This preconceived notion emanates from a belief that it is the pitch that determines the trajectory and direction of the baseball off the bat. I believe this to be incorrect. Instead it is the **swing path** and <u>not</u> the **pitch** that determines the trajectory of the ball off of the bat. As we will see from the following examples, the hitters with the highest batting averages are the ones that are successful with low pitches and who use a swing path that allows them to hit low pitches hard and/or elevate them.

Modern technology and an army of statisticians record every aspect of every pitch thrown in major league baseball. Every conceivable nugget of information is recorded going well beyond velocity. Today's technology records the velocity at different stages of the pitch (release point, home plate, etc. down to a tenth of a mile per hour), pitch type, pitch trajectory, the count when a type of pitch was thrown, the location and result. The result is not recorded merely as an out or a hit, but with specificity down to type of trajectory off the bat (groundball, line drive, fly ball and pop-up), where the hit landed on the field and the pitch count of each hit. For my purposes, I focus on the pitch location, the result (i.e. was it a ground ball, fly ball, etc.) and success (which is measure by batting average). Unless indicated otherwise, all of the following data is from *brooksbaseball.net*. Let's look at some examples:

Dustin Pedroia

Dustin Pedroia stands at 5 feet 8 inches, hits right-handed and is a regular All-Star second baseman for the Boston Red Sox. In 2013, Pedroia hit .301 overall, saw 2,934 pitches, had 619 official at-bats and 185 hits.

As indicated next, of all pitches thrown to Pedroia, 29% were in the upper most portion of the zone or above; 47% were in the lower most portion of the zone or below; and 24% were thrown in the middle part of the zone. Each of the previous pitching percentages include pitches thrown outside the strike zone. Almost half of the pitches thrown to him are low **or below** the strike zone and, therefore, he must be successful with these pitches in order to hit over .300. In fact, 100 of his 185 hits (54%) came from pitches in these two low zones (especially on the inside portion of those zones). His total batting average for the lowest two zones was **.340**. His total batting average for the top two zones was **.212**. His batting average for the middle zone was **.298**. For Pedroia, he was far more successful hitting in the zones that are considered the "pitcher's spots" than in the areas most often thought of as a batter's spot (i.e. the upper part of the zone). The following is a table showing all pitches thrown to Dustin Pedroia in the 2013 regular season by location (catcher's point of view) with the "strike zone" identified in bold:

Hitting Low in the Zone: A New Baseball Paradigm

14%	17%	22%	23%	24%		
74	74	75	58	69		12%
79	100	107	113	88		17%
95	110	164	182	142		24%
66	107	159	144	136		21%
89	98	132	183	204		26%

The table below shows Pedroia's batting average in each of the hitting zone locations from the 2013 regular season (with hits/ABs noted in the margins):

25/83 .301	53/152 .349	58/188 .308	39/147 .265	10/49 .204		
.000	.222	.214	.000	.000		5/31 .161
.222	.355	.219	.100	.000		24/106 .226
.242	.366	.291	.350	.158		56/188 .298
.476	.395	.392	.277	.286		62/171 .362
.333	.303	.333	.286	.300		38/123 .309

Why was Pedroia successful in the lowest two zones in 2013?[14] Almost half of the pitches he saw were "low" in **his** hitting zone, and he was less successful with pitches up in the zone. It became clear to me after studying and breaking down hours of Pedroia's video that he was able to elevate low pitches for line drives or produce hard hit ground balls that got through the infield for base hits instead of weak rollovers. It is easy to assume that because he's shorter than the average major league player that some of his success could have been attributed to his stature. Pedroia's lack of height is an advantage when hitting low in the zone, but his success was a direct result of having the proper mechanics and swing path to accommodate the low pitches. Pedroia's spray charts from 2013 tell the story. Look at where and how he is getting his hits. Since the vast majority of his hits are coming from the lowest part of the zone, Pedroia must elevate the pitches to carry them to the outfield as often as possible. Conversely, you will see that most of his outs are ground balls to the left side.

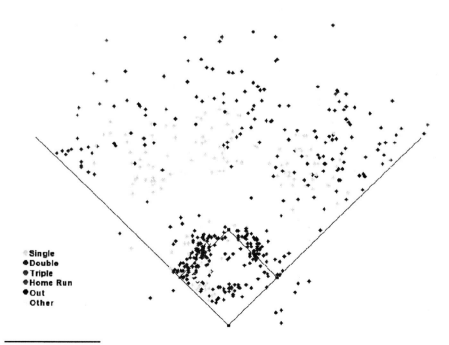

14 Dustin Pedroia suffered a wrist injury in 2014 requiring surgery making a comparison to 2013 not reliable.

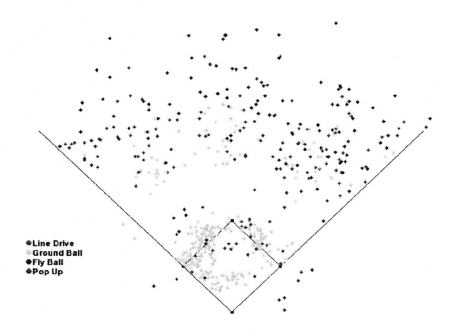

Mike Trout

    Mike Trout stands at 6 feet 2 inches, hits right-handed and plays outfield for the Anaheim Angels. He is widely considered to be an up-and-coming superstar in the game. In 2013, he batted .318 overall, saw 2,942 pitches, had 581 at-bats with 185 hits. Trout had 27 home runs, 97 RBI and led the American League in runs scored (109). Following is a table showing all pitches thrown to Mike Trout in the 2013 regular season by location (catcher's point of view) with the "strike zone" identified in bold:

Hitting Low in the Zone: A New Baseball Paradigm

19%	17%	20%	21%	23%		
82	53	64	52	45		10%
98	106	85	80	78		15%
119	128	143	140	147		23%
138	110	169	169	172		26%
120	104	142	167	231		26%

The next table shows Trout's batting averages in each of the hitting zone locations from the 2013 regular season (with hits/ABs noted in the margins):

33/89 .370	50/143 .350	51/138 .370	38/139 .273	13/72 .181		
.000	.000	.000	.000	.000		0/14 .000
.077	.273	.182	.167	.333		16/75 .213
.333	.367	.333	.381	.150		59/177 .333
.484	.405	.479	.241	.167		72/197 .365
.467	.400	.389	.240	.185		38/118 .322

Hitting Low in the Zone: A New Baseball Paradigm

I have highlighted the bottom two zones to demonstrate that 110 of Mike Trout's 185 hits (60%) come from these two areas. Like Pedroia, Mike Trout sees almost half of his pitches "low" in **his** hitting zone, and he is less successful in pitches in the uppermost part of the zone. Despite the difference in their physical statures, Trout also uses a swing path that allows him to drive low pitches for line drives and hard-hit ground ball base hits rather than weak rollovers. Taller hitters do need to make a slight downward adjustment when hitting low in the zone to reach the most pitches. Again, Trout's spray charts tell the story. Look at where and how he is getting his hits. Since the vast majority of his hits are coming from the lowest part of the zone, Trout elevates pitches to carry them to the outfield. Conversely, you will see that most of his outs are ground balls to the left side. See Trout's spray charts for 2013 and 2014…

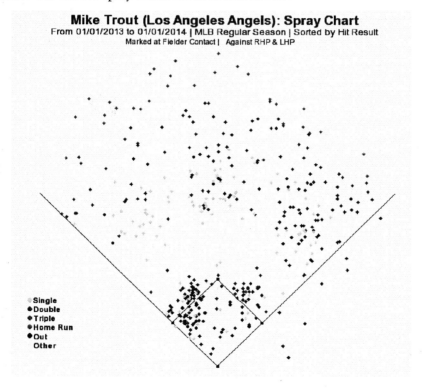

Hitting Low in the Zone: A New Baseball Paradigm

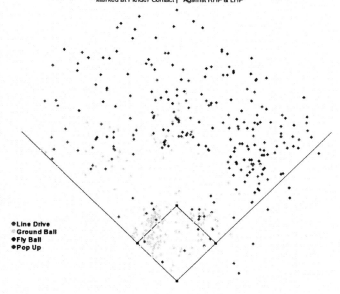

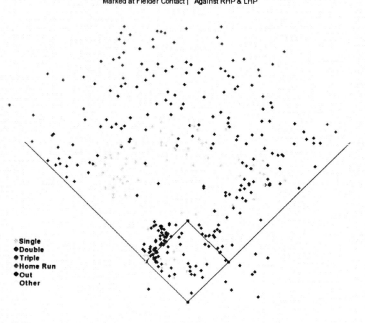

Hitting Low in the Zone: A New Baseball Paradigm

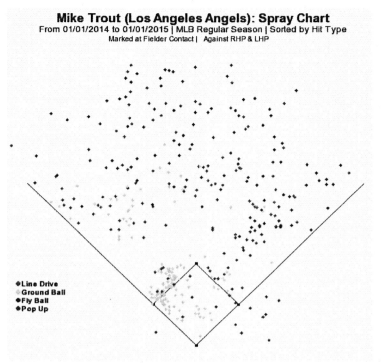

Statistical Comparison
Mike Trout 2013 vs. 2014

A side by side comparison of the two seasons is revealing:

	2013	**2014**	**Difference**
Overall Average	.318	.287	(.031)
Overall Hits	184	173	(11)
At Bats	581	602	21
Pitches Seen	2,942	3,160	218
Volume of Pitches (Top to Bottom)			
	10%	12%	2%
	15%	17%	2%
	23%	24%	1%
	26%	22%	(4%)
	26%	25%	(1%)

Hitting Low in the Zone: A New Baseball Paradigm

	2013	**2014**	**Difference**
Hits by Zone (Top to Bottom)			
	0	0	-
	16	10	(6)
	59	58	(1)
	72	74	2
	38	37	(1)
Swings by Zone (Top to Bottom)			
	23	39	16
	142	224	82
	316	359	43
	354	331	(23)
	269	253	(16)
Outcomes			
Singles	115	89	(26)
Doubles	39	39	-
Triples	9	9	-
Homeruns	27	36	9
Walks	110	83	(27)
Strikeouts	136	184	48
Groundouts	131	100	(31)
Air Outs	148	161	13

Trout's 2014 season was significantly different from 2013 in a number of ways — most notable, the 31 point drop-off in his batting average and fewer hits despite having more at-bats. There is no one thing that can be pointed to as the cause. But a few things can be observed. First, as a result of Trout's success in the lower part of the zone in 2013, teams appeared to stay away from those areas more often as can be seen in the 5% decrease in pitches thrown in the lowest two hitting zones. Second, Trout swung more often at pitches up in the hitting zone and swung at fewer pitches in the lower part. I submit that it is not a coincidence that his productivity in the upper parts of the zone dropped as a result of more swing attempts in those same areas. Third, while Trout's overall hits dropped, the number of home runs hit jumped by 30%. Now maybe Trout muscled up too much this year and was trying to hit home runs by chasing after the high pitches, or maybe he lost patience looking for pitches low in the zone. I did watch him in a few of the 2014 playoff games and saw a few weak pop-ups to the right side of the infield on high pitches. Who knows the exact answer? But we know Mike Trout is a good player and too sound mechanically not to make the right adjustment. But I believe that the answer for him and most players lies in being patient to get good pitches to hit low in the zone and use the right swing path. While Trout saw 5% fewer pitches in the two lowest parts of the zone in 2014 than he did in 2013, still 47% (nearly half) of the pitches thrown to him were in those two zones which left plenty of opportunities for him to hit.

Trout's production was the subject of a recent article by Jeff Sullivan at FoxSports.com.[15] In his article, Sullivan observed that the league had made a general shift of pitching lower in the zone than it had in years past. He believes Mike Trout was seeing an exaggerated proportion of these pitches. He noted, as I did previously, that while Mike Trout continued to hit effectively in the lower part of the zone, his production was falling off in the upper part. Sullivan wrote:

> *The general message being sent: Mike Trout has been absolutely killing pitches down in and beyond the zone. Yet, he's been struggling against pitches up... Against pitches in the lower third of the strike zone this year, Trout's slugged a spectacular .875. Against pitches in the upper third of the strike zone this year, Trout's slugged a*

---

15 Jeff Sullivan, "*Why Mike Trout – And the Rest of the League – Is Having Trouble with the High Stuff,*" *Foxsports.com*, August 29, 2014, http://www.foxsports.com/mlb/just-a-bit-outside/story/why-mike-trout-and-the-rest-of-the-league-is-having-trouble-with-the-high-stuff.

feeble .211. The former is among the best in the league. The latter's among the very worst... And despite what the numbers say, Trout's seen more low pitches than high pitches. To this point, 11 percent of his pitches have been in that upper third. And 14 percent have been in the bottom third. It seems odd, but Trout is just an extreme example of a league-wide trend.

Statistical Comparison Trout vs. Pedroia

Let's go back to the 2013 season and compare the two hitters we've discussed side-by-side. They are very different people physically, but in 2013, they both had the same number of hits, while seeing virtually the same number of pitches.

	Trout	**Pedroia**	**Pedroia**
Overall Avg.	.318	.301	.017
Overall Hits	184	185	(1)
At-bats	581	619	(34)
Pitches Seen	2,942	2,934	8
Volume of Pitches (Top to Bottom)			
	10%	12%	(2%)
	15%	17%	(2%)
	23%	24%	(1%)
	26%	21%	5%
	26%	26%	-
Hits by Zone (Top to Bottom)			
	0	5	(5)
	16	24	(8)
	59	56	3
	72	62	10
	38	38	-

What jumps off the page for me is that in 2013, both Mike Trout and Dustin Pedroia had 100 and 110, respectively, of their hits come from the bottom two hitting zones. That's 60% of Trout's total hits and 54% of Pedroia's hits coming from the lowest two hitting zones in 2013, and both batting nearly .350 in those zones. In 2014, Trout collected even more hits in the lowest two portions of the zone and these hits were a larger percentage of his overall hits – because he had fewer hits (111 hits, 64% of all hits). So even when they tried to pitch away from Trout's strength, he actually did even better in that area. I am convinced that if Mike Trout "zoned down" even more and forced pitchers to come to his zone (rather than taking what they give him) his production will return to past levels.

Chapter 4

A Universal Approach to Hitting: Preparation, Focus and Execution

What makes an average hitter good and a good hitter great? There is no single answer. The baseball swing has too many interdependent pieces, and there are too many variables in the game for us to select one single piece. In addition, an individual players' approach to hitting and ability to focus with intensity (and not lose himself in the moment) plays a significant part. However, it would make sense that the players who demonstrated the greatest success at the plate over long periods of time have similarities in their approach and swing. I believe that a consistent "approach" to hitting allows hitters (those who are great and those who want to be great) to place themselves in a situation where they can repeat solid mechanics over and over again.

People often say that baseball players are superstitious (e.g. they won't step on chalk lines or talk to a pitcher who is throwing a no-hitter) or that they are obsessive (e.g. only eating certain types of food before a game or placing socks on the same way every time). There may be truth to both of these. But I think at the root of this behavior, players are searching for a routine or an approach that allows them to manage what they are capable of controlling in hopes of repeating themselves and achieving success over and over again. Seriously, does anybody really think that Wade Boggs, one of the purest hitters in the history of the game, would have been a .235 career hitter if he ate steak once in a while before a game? Of course not. But his approach of eating chicken before **every** game helped him be in a place where **he** felt in control and was able to repeat his success with great volume. And that's what all players strive for in the game.

So what do I mean by having an "approach?" In essence, I mean three things: (1) preparation; (2) focus; and (3) execution. And these three things are steps toward a goal: to consistently hit well with a repeatable swing that is grooved thousands of times for every one actual swing in the batter's box.

The player with the best overall approach I have ever seen is, without out a doubt, Derek Jeter. I had the privilege of playing with him in 1997, 1998, and 2004, and let me tell you, he is the real deal. The name of the game is consistent production, so who better to highlight than *The Captain*. In nineteen years with the Yankees, he appeared in fourteen All-Star Games, won five Gold Glove Awards, won five Silver Slugger Awards, hit over .300 twelve times, had a career batting average of .310, accumulated 3,465 career hits (6th all-time), had eight 200+ hit seasons (career average of 204 hits per season), a postseason batting average of .308 across 650 official at-bats and racked up five World Series titles in seven appearances. These Hall of Fame worthy numbers don't just happen. They are the product of a highly disciplined and methodical person who prepares for every moment with intense focus and who repeatedly executes his game plan at the plate. The proof is in his spray chart (see Jeter's spray charts). His outs are generally ground balls to shortstop or second base and most of his hits are center and right center field in beautiful bunches.[16] You don't get clusters of success like his over a twenty year period by flying by the seat of your pants. Jeter was consistent and proved his worth by repeating his process over and over again: perfecting that famous inside-out swing while lacing balls to right-field. He is certain to be a first-ballot Hall of Famer not because he hit the most home runs or stole the most bases. He belongs there because he, like most of the inductees, was consistently excellent for nearly twenty years. I leave it up to the Baseball Writers Association of America whether he should be the first player inducted by a unanimous vote but, given how he has lived his life on and off the field, it would be appropriate if they did so.

---

16 Brooksbaseball data only goes back to 2007, and therefore a complete spray chart of Jeter's career was not possible.

Hitting Low in the Zone: A New Baseball Paradigm

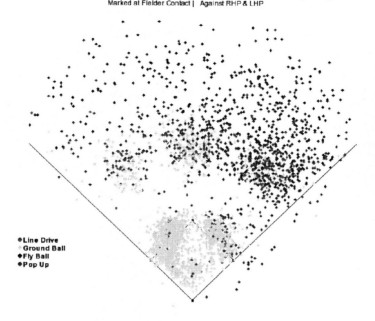

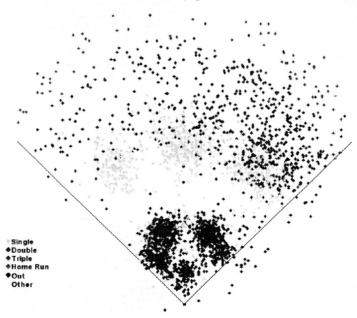

Hitting Low in the Zone: A New Baseball Paradigm

Preparation:

Let's start with what you can do before you pick up a bat. First things first: be prepared physically. Today's ballplayers are bigger and stronger than they were thirty years ago, and the game demands both strength and speed to excel at higher levels. But even on a day-to-day basis, the long grind of a season demands that players be in top physical shape. Players that are out of shape usually get hurt or lose their jobs to more fit prospects that have the potential to stay off the disabled list.

Preparation also means doing your homework. With today's technology, every pitch of every game is recorded. Not just on videotape but with high-tech sensors that measure velocity, break, location, etc. down to ridiculously minute details. I was taught the importance of studying video by one of the best, Tony Gwynn. He taught me how to break down a video to see what I was doing right and wrong. He preached making adjustments from at-bat to at-bat not just game to game. There is no shortage of information at the professional level that a hitter, wanting to get better, can't study to find some edge or to discover a habit that tips a pitch. It's truly an example of "how much you put in is how much you get out." I think most players today take advantage of the resources available to them. At the Little League and high school levels, technology isn't as widely available, but it is still possible to look for an edge. Your opponent warms up right in front of you. Baseball is a game where finding little edges can make a big difference. But if you won't put in the work, don't expect to find the edge.

Repetition is also a part of preparation. This starts with how you practice your swing and how you prepare for each game. Name some of the current players who you consider elite hitters. Who you name may depend upon who your favorite team is, but objectively you would have to consider the following names in the conversation: Mike Trout, Derek Jeter and Dustin Pedroia. Now, picture in your head one of their at-bats. Can you see how they dig in? How they wiggle the bat? Their swing? Their finish? And maybe even some idiosyncrasy they have (*Derek Jeter asking for time and tugging on the brim of his helmet; Dustin Pedroia endlessly fixing his batting gloves*). These are triggers that help them get ready. Do you know why you can picture it? Because, if you follow that player, you have watched hundreds of their at-bats and they do the same thing every time, and the best hitters seek to repeat the same swing over and over again to find consistency. Rarely will you see a hitter change his batting stance and swing in any way noticeable to the masses.

Focus:

Sounds easy, but it's not. I have never seen anyone more focused and disciplined than Hideki Matsui. I had the opportunity of playing with him in 2004. His focus started the moment he arrived at the ballpark. He had the same pre-game routine most days which led to his approach in the batter's box. From how he stepped in the box, and how he held the bat, to how he checked his hands to make sure everything was in order before he proceeded—he was all business. In my opinion, his focus was so intense that nothing could distract him from the immediate task ahead of him. It's that kind of intense, unwavering focus that made him elite in both Japan and the United States.

When we talk about focus, I must mention one of the greatest second basemen to play the game, Roberto Alomar. I've gotten to know Roberto very well over the past few years while coaching with him at the annual Toronto Blue Jays Honda Super Camps that are held all across Canada. I once asked him why he was such a better player than I was, and he chuckled and replied, "I always knew what I wanted to do on the baseball field." He went on to say that on defense he usually knew exactly where he wanted to position himself for most hitters, and at the plate he consistently looked for the ball "down and in." With that type of laser focus, Alomar always managed to make the game look easy.

Now, what can we do as hitters to be more focused? The number one goal of a hitter is to not give away at-bats. Let's look at three things a hitter can work on to improve mental focus at the plate:

1. Don't be afraid to take pitches: As a batter, if you're looking for a pitch in a certain area (low in the zone) and you don't get it, you have to be disciplined enough to TAKE IT.

2. No guessing: Don't try to guess pitches. Batters are often guilty of trying to anticipate the pitch instead of just reacting to what they see. Especially before two strikes, if you're looking for a pitch down, you can't find yourself swinging at a pitch up.

3. Stay in the moment: If you've ever been a two-hole hitter, you'll relate to this one. You often find yourself watching the base runner instead of focusing on pitches. Focus on the task at hand.

Execution:

Execution in its simplest form is the act of carrying out what you've practiced or learned. I have to once again fall back on Derek Jeter. I often think about Jeter and his approach, and I try to instill his approach to execution into young players including my own son. When thinking about all of the big moments in Jeter's career, whether it was regular season, All-Star play or postseason, it required a high level of concentration and focus to execute at the plate. It wasn't luck. It was just fitting for him to execute excellence one more time in his final at-bat at Yankee Stadium in 2014 with a walk-off base hit to right field. People sometimes say that Jeter is overrated and that his popularity was driven by the New York stage. I believe his ability to execute his game plan at the plate, time and time again, in spite of the bright lights, is what makes him one of the best players of all time.

On a much smaller level, when I was the hitting coach for the Eugene Emeralds in 2014—a minor league affiliate of the San Diego Padres—I would often emphasize to the players the importance of knowing what they want to do at the plate, staying in the moment and executing their plan. When our mid-season additions (the Padres' new draft picks), joined us they got off to a slow start. I knew I had to get a message across to them, so I pulled them aside to offer some guidance and let them know that they were too talented to keep making the same mistakes and that they needed to work on doing a better job of executing. Their main focus had to be on their swing paths and pitch location.

When it comes to the importance of execution, one player in particular comes to mind from that season, Auston Bousfield. Bousfield was a fourth round pick from Ole Miss and a very good player. But he struggled a bit in the beginning. Once trust was established between us, I worked with him to focus on the same elements: pitch trajectory, pitch location and his swing path. Bousfield, along with many of the other players excelled. It was noticeable and immediate. He went from hitting .180 to as high as .335 and finished the season at .300. Like most good hitting coaches, I worked with what he had and tried to bring out his best to maximize his capabilities. He, like the others, were all elite athletes who had years of training and have taken thousands of swings, so with the right understanding of pitch trajectory and swing path they all had the potential to succeed.

Part III

Swing Mechanics

Chapter 5

The Game Plan

Now we get to the fun part: swing mechanics. A player's hitting mechanics need to generate two things: they need to focus on getting the ball in the air as much as possible, and they need to effectively promote the most coverage of the hitting zone from the ground up. The mechanics designed for an upward swing path will maximize a hitter's chances for sustained success in both of these areas. And that swing path shouldn't change—regardless of the situation. Successful hitting has often been said to be achieved through luck. This couldn't be further from the truth. As hitters, we must eliminate the concept of luck from our minds. The player's ability to stay in the moment and execute under pressure is extremely important for hit production and when driving in runs. Good hitters thrive under pressure because they have a plan, then they execute that plan no matter how big the moment. Dr. Bob Rotella, in his golf book *Your 15th Club*, writes about the importance of being repetitive with your mechanics and having a clear mind no matter the situation or the opponent. When I reflect back on my career, I can't count the number of at-bats I gave away when facing big time pitchers like Pedro Martinez or Roger Clemens because I was always focusing on trying to do well, not missing my pitch or staying away from the pitcher's best pitch. As a batter, your job is to know your swing path and to execute it over and over again. When there are runners on base, a pitcher is more likely to throw low in the zone in hopes of inducing a ground ball out. In that moment it is especially important to stay disciplined and swing up at the ball to get it elevated into the air.

Why does the ball need to be in the air? Balls hit in the air are much more productive than ground balls. Remember, the pitcher wants you to hit a ground ball somewhere in the infield: there are four infielders and only three outfielders;

balls hit on the ground don't go over the fence for home runs; players have beat out ground balls to be safe at first, but I've never heard of anyone getting a double or triple on a ground ball to the infield. Balls hit in the air to the outfield can fall between the infielder and the outfielder; get hit hard in the gaps; rattle around in the corners; fly over the fence with or without a bounce and, sometimes, can fall into an outfielder's glove but still allow a run to score from third base after tagging up. What we can see from the analysis above is that scoring runs is much more efficient with extra-base hits because the batter will finish in scoring position and he himself can score on a hit, extra-base hit or sacrifice fly.

Secondly, your swing mechanics need to enable you to cover as much area as possible from the ground up to below the belt. In order for a hitter to hit for high average, have extra-base hits or to drive in tons of runs, he needs lots of opportunities. High average hitters need anywhere from 170-200 hits over the course of a season. What I've come to realize through my research is looking for strikes over the heart of the plate just leaves a hitter coming up short. Now, knowing that hitters need this certain production, where can they get it? Where are the most opportunities? There are only two choices: above or below the strike zone. The most viable option is below. It is also important to note that the lower the pitch, the more productive the fly ball. Higher pitches will yield weak pop flies even if you have the correct swing path unless you're able to catch them way out front. Lower pitches allow the bat to travel further which generates more bat speed and leads to more line drives and extra-base hits. Whether a result of the opposing pitcher's game plan or the effects of gravity, the highest majority of pitches are sinking, so hitting low in the zone is the best counter action for a hitter.

Let's recall the article on FoxSports.com from 2014 by Jeff Sullivan on Mike Trout seeing more pitches low in the zone. Sullivan later noted the connection between low pitches, swing path and building teams.

> *So targets get set low, and the pitches follow. Hitters have tried to respond, and they've had some modest success. You can believe me, or you can believe a real-life MLB front office. See, this isn't my discovery. This is me taking the long way to point at someone else's work. From a recent Business Week Astros profile:*
>
> > *Everybody says, 'Keep the ball down, keep the ball down, "says [Brent] Strom. Major league teams have long favored ground-ball pitchers,*

> since grounders tend not to result in doubles, triples, or home runs."

> But here again, advanced data yielded a useful insight: Major league hitters had become so adept at hitting low pitches that they were vulnerable to high ones. [Oakland A's GM Billy Beane] had discovered a particularly clever countermove. Beane stayed ahead of the curve," says Strom, by finding hitters with a steep upward swing path to counter the sinking action of pitchers trying to induce ground balls."

> Billy Beane put together a baseball team constructed to fight those low pitches. That was part of the response. Because of the response, the upper parts of the zone have opened up again, because only the best hitters in the league are really capable of controlling all sides. The Astros had Collin McHugh start to throw more elevated four-seam fastballs, on the idea that he could zig where other pitchers continue to zag. McHugh is having an outstanding season out of nowhere, with more strike outs than innings, and 18 percent of his two-strike fastballs have generated strikeouts.

> So this is how we proceed in the league's hunt for equilibrium. For years, pitchers worked to throw down more and more often. There was a greater emphasis placed on generating grounders and avoiding balls in the air. The league has started to respond, with hitters focusing more on making good contact with those low pitches. And also with teams focusing more on finding hitters with the right swing paths. Now, for the first time we know of, hitters are slugging better against low pitches than high pitches. So now the league will eventually respond to the response, re-establishing the upper parts of the zone. McHugh is one example, but it seems it'll be a while yet before more pitchers resume elevating. For now, they're still doing what they've always been told, and they're pitching to their own strengths instead of to the hitters' weaknesses.[17]

The part of Jeff Sullivan's article on the Oakland A's really struck me, and after studying nearly every MLB team's roster, data, tendencies, and video, the A's stood out the most. I found that the A's had more swing activity 2 ½ feet down in the hitting zone than almost any other team. They had the least amount of swing activity up in the zone of nearly all the teams. That led me to believe through

---

[17] Jeff Sullivan, "Why *Mike Trout – And the Rest of the League – Is Having Trouble with the High Stuff,*" *FoxSports.com,* Aug 29, 2014, http://www.foxsports.com/mlb/just-a-bit-outside/story/why-mike-trout-and-the-rest-of-the-league-is-having-trouble-with-the-high-stuff.

luck or philosophy that they were zoning down and taking high pitches. Their high extra-base hit production led me to the video, which is where I observed the consistent steep uppercut swings throughout the lineup used to elevate those low pitches. Do I believe that Billy Beane built a team with a certain swing path? Probably not. But I wouldn't be surprised if he did. Billy Beane has proven year after year that he's a brilliant baseball mind, and he knows how to implement his game plan with patience and precision. But one thing I am certain of is that in order for the A's to repeatedly elevate low pitches, the hitters must have similarities in their mechanics and swing path. The numbers don't lie. In 2014, the A's had the most triples in the American League (33), were 8th in home runs (146) and, perhaps most importantly, 4th in runs scored (729). [18] In 2013 the A's had more extra-base hits than everyone else and were also able to keep runs scored against them down by acquiring pitchers who could keep the ball down and thereby generate a lot of ground-ball outs.

Andrew Koo wrote an article for BaseballProspectus.com in 2013 on the Oakland A's purposely acquiring fly-ball hitters. See the following findings:

Year	Team	FB_PA%	Wins
2013	OAK	59.8	96
2010	ARI	42.0	65
2011	TOR	40.0	81
2013	BOS	39.5	97
2008	ARI	38.7	82
2013	SEA	38.1	71
2009	PHI	37.3	93
2011	ARI	36.9	94
2010	NYA	36.3	95
2010	TOR	36.2	85
2005	TEX	36.0	79

18   www.mlb.com

It is no coincidence that no other team has even come close to Oakland's almost 60% plate appearances by fly-ball hitters in nearly a decade.[19] This data just further proves the importance of getting the ball in the air on a consistent basis.

Most hitting philosophies will produce some level of success for a player in the beginning. But what I want to stress is the philosophy that I advocate in this book maximizes **consistent** success for a hitter. Surely, hitters have different abilities and one size does not fit all. But I do think it makes a whole lot of sense to have a swing that is designed to make contact where the overwhelming majority of pitches are thrown – and not the fewest. The mechanics discussed later will give hitters the best chance to be successful at the plate in large volumes over a long period of time.

But, before we start any discussion about swing mechanics, we need to define what we are trying to achieve at the plate. As I have discussed extensively, we are looking for balls to be hit in the air. Ground balls to the infield never result in doubles or triples. We want balls hit in the air over the infield, in the gaps or over the wall. We want balls that can result in hits, extra-base hits or runs being scored via sac flies.

---

19 Andrew Koo, "*More Money Ball: Oakland's Other Platoon Advantage,*" Baseball Prospectus.com, December 18, 2013, http://www.baseballprospectus.com/article.php?articleid=22435.

Chapter 6

The Grip and Stance

The grip on the baseball bat and the stance go together. It is important to think about the grip and stance being built from the bottom up. Hitters get so focused on bat speed and hands that they forget that your feet positioning in your batting stance is what determines your ability to effectively cover larger areas of the hitting zone. **THIS IS EXTREMELY IMPORTANT!** Your feet control your hands. I subscribe to the conventional idea that knees should be slightly flexed and feet parallel or front foot slightly forward towards the plate.

But how and where you hold the bat is equally important. Start with the hands low and the barrel of the bat upright with relaxed fingers. How your hands settle naturally will determine your grip. A loose and comfortable grip: (a) makes it easier for the hitter to control the barrel of the bat at all times, (b) allows the batter to maximize bat speed, and (c) ultimately produces a quality load. The batting stance serves one main purpose: to transition the body into the load as seamlessly as possible. Andrew McCutchen of the Pittsburgh Pirates does this very well (see photo 1).

Above all, the hands need to be relaxed—especially the top one. Tight hands and forearms create resistance and work against having a quality load. I used to train with Desai Williams, the former Olympic sprinter from Canada, and he would say *a loose muscle was a fast muscle and a tight muscle was a slow muscle.* While I don't think his swing should be emulated, Kevin Youkilis kept his top hand off the bat until the last second and had one of the quickest bats in baseball.

Andrew McCutchen demonstrating the proper grip and stance.

PHOTO CREDIT: GETTY IMAGES

Chapter 7

The Load

In my opinion, the load is the most important aspect of hitting. The load produces the coiled body force that is necessary for an explosive, powerful swing and gets the batter in attack mode. A batter loads when the pitcher begins his wind-up. I was always taught that the load was necessary for timing, rhythm and to help the batter keep his hands back. I've since found that a proper load enhances balance, maximizes power generation and promotes a batter's swing path. And this is especially important since we now know that the swing path determines how much of the hitting zone a batter can cover. The following steps happen simultaneously:

1. The front foot steps slightly forward a few inches and a little towards the plate. When the foot comes down, the toe should still be facing the plate like it was in your original stance. If the foot opens up even a little, you're leaking oil and you've weakened your hitting position. This is not a "dive" but a slight step forward and toward the plate. The front leg will be used during the swing as the pivot, so it is important to keep it strong and firm.

2. The front shoulder should angle slightly down and back. The downward tilt will allow for the upward tick in the swing (discussed next). The slight move back creates torque to be unleashed during the swing and at impact. This is important because keeping your shoulders square will promote a level swing which leads to ground ball outcomes.

3. The hands and the back elbow will lift slightly to permit the bat to settle behind the helmet and neck. This is what most hitters refer to as "wrapping." Wrapping has long been thought of as a bad thing. But on the contrary, wrapping is of major importance because it's the only way to build up bat speed (See Mike Trout in the photo 2). This is the only time when screaming, "Elbow up, buddy!" to your son at his Little League game is relevant. The proper time for this is during the load, not the stance. Don't feel bad if you've been guilty of yelling this from time to time. I heard it constantly growing up and still hear parents screaming it from the stands today.

Mike Trout exhibiting the perfect Load.

PHOTO CREDIT: GETTY IMAGES

Chapter 8

The Swing Path

This is where the rubber meets the road. It is the swing path (not the pitch) that will dictate the direction and flight of the baseball. Therefore, the correct swing path must be applied if we want to elevate the ball on a consistent basis. I believe a swing path with a slight upward trajectory is best. We have previously established that almost all pitches have a downward trajectory. Therefore, we are looking to reverse it and send it back from whence it came. I don't see how a pitch moving downward can be consistently elevated by a corresponding downward swing. I know that the common thinking is that a downward swing will create back-spin for a fly ball and, presumably, power for home runs or hard hit grounders that get through for hits. This is just nonsense. It is physically impossible for this to be the case. In order for a hitter to consistently elevate pitches into the air, the correct swing has to be in the form of an arc with a slight upward trajectory.

Ted Williams, arguably the greatest hitter ever, said flat out that an upswing is the correct path. In his book, *The Science of Hitting*, Ted Williams makes the point, succinctly, that a slight upswing is the best swing because: (a) it promotes balls hit in the air with power and authority; and (b) pitchers throw the ball low and therefore an upswing is necessary to drive the ball into the air.

> *Now, what about that "level" swing? As I said, you have always heard that the ideal swing is level or "down". Your swing often coincides with your capabilities . . . . A fly ball from a light hitter*

is usually an out. When the ball is on the ground, it puts greater burden on the fielders. Things can happen.

But if you get the ball in the air with power, you have the gift to produce the most important hit in baseball – the home run. More importantly is that you hit consistently with authority. For those purposes, I advocate a slight upswing (from level to about 10 degrees), and there is another good reason for this – the biggest reason:

Say the average pitcher is 6 foot 2. He's standing on a mound 10 inches high. He's pitching overhand or three-quarter arm. He releases the ball right about ear level. Your strike zone is, roughly, from 22 inches to 4 feet 8. Most pitchers will come in below the waist, because the low pitches are tough to hit. The flight of the ball is down . . . about 5 degrees. A slight upswing – again, led by the hips coming around and up – puts the bat flush in line with the path of the ball for a longer period – that 12- to 18-inch impact zone. [20]

But hitters—especially at the professional level—will see many more low pitches than elevated "mistakes" and those low pitches can and should be feasted on, which will greatly improve the hitter's statistical performance. You've heard announcers say many times (and perhaps you've experienced it yourself) that a hitter's eyes get big when he is thrown a high pitch. Why? Conventional wisdom says that those pitches are easier to see and therefore hitters are more likely to swing at them. But many hitters have been told for a long time that low pitches can't be hit with power and elevated for home runs on a consistent basis. I like to think of high pitches as a bacon double cheeseburger with a side of fries. It tastes really good, but isn't healthy for you at all! With a swing grooved to handle low pitches, it will be easier for hitters to pass up the waist-high or above fastball.

So how do we get that upward trajectory in our swing? Most of the hard work has already been done in the load.

- As a hitter you are trying to stay inside the ball, therefore the swing is driven by the torso and the knob of the bat.
- With the front shoulder tilted, the torso turns with the knob of the bat coming underneath your body and the barrel of the bat points downward (See Mike Trout photo 3).

---

20 Ted Williams, *The Science of Hitting* (New York: Touchstone, 2013), 49-50.

Hitting Low in the Zone: A New Baseball Paradigm

- Because the torso and hands are driving the knob through, the barrel head stays in the hitting zone longer.

- The barrel then travels upward and along the line of your feet into the ball, creating a swing path. The bat literally needs to sweep through the hitting zone to increase chances of contact.

- Contact with the ball is in the middle of your body—not out in front. All of your dynamic energy is being concentrated on a single spot at the apex of the swing arc. Contact too early or too late results in less force at impact.

Mike Trout has one of the best Swing Paths in the game.

PHOTO CREDIT: GETTY IMAGES

Swing path determines where the ball will end up out in the field. Deeper contact will send the ball to right field. Contact closer to the center of your body will send the ball to center field. And if the hitter makes contact with the ball out front, it will go to left field.

Hitters cannot be self-proclaimed pull hitters or opposite field hitters unless they know how the bat and ball react to one another. Pull hitters hit for low average, have low extra-base hits and drive in less runs. They also hit more ground balls and have fewer at-bats. This affects the whole team because it stops the line from moving and leads to less opportunities at the plate. Opposite field hitters like Trout and Jeter tend to have high base-hit production and better on-base percentage which leads to more runs scored and higher possibility for postseason appearances.

A little something to think about…

Similar to golf, everyone needs to have about the same approach at contact when hitting. There are not hundreds of ways to hit a golf ball. The same is true with baseball. There needs to be similarities in the swing path of different hitters to handle the trajectory and speeds of the various pitches. A hitter cannot just hit the ball any old way and expect it to do what he wants it to do. A line drive swing and home run swing are the same swing—just different body positioning. I don't care what you do to the ball after the point of contact; it will not affect how far the ball goes. There is no such thing as hitting through the baseball. Once contact is made, the bat and ball separate. It is the bat speed that's built up **BEFORE** contact that determines how far the ball will fly. Robert Adair, Ph.D. describes this perfectly in his book *The Physics of Baseball* where he states… *"The course of the swing after the ball is struck is kinematically irrelevant. The emphasis by coaches and sports teachers on the 'follow-through' in baseball (and golf and tennis, among other sports) is designed to ensure proper actions* **before** *the ball is struck."* [21] This is especially important to understand because it confirms that hitting is about angles and physics not swinging level like we were all taught as youngsters. Now, isn't that amazing! It is impossible for me to put into writing everything that I've learned about hitting through research, observation, and experience over the years. It is way too complicated. Besides it would be downright foolish of me to tell all of my secrets, but for the sake of this book, I am divulging enough information to

---

21 Robert K. Adair, Ph.D., *The Physics of Baseball*, (New York: It Books, 1990), 36.

simply open up a conversation on what it actually takes to have repeated success at the plate as a hitter. I am aware that change is not always easy, but with the adjustments mentioned, a hitter will reap huge dividends. I'm confident that if a batter focuses on the three areas outlined: grip/stance, load and swing path, he will see drastic and immediate improvement in production.

In 2014, as the batting coach to the Eugene Emeralds, I witnessed first-hand how taking aim at the lower part of the hitting zone with the proper swing path could be effective. Although it was only a 76 game season, the team improved in every offensive category. That year, the Emeralds led the league in home runs (50 – the most hit by any Emeralds team since moving into the pitcher-friendly PK Park in 2010) and doubles (151 – the most hit by the Emeralds since 2006). I was so confident in my philosophy with this group of talented young men that I guaranteed them that if they trusted me and executed, we would double the home run production of the previous season. And we were only four shy of doing just that. They had hit 27 home runs in 2013. The team also improved in every offensive statistic compared to the prior season: runs, hits, team batting average, on-base percentage, slugging percentage and on-base plus slugging percentage. In fact, it was the most production the team had in years. What was the difference? Our offense focused down in the hitting zone and got the ball in the air.

So many of these young men benefitted from the information I brought to the table, but there are two in particular that I'd like to mention: Marcus Davis and Trea Turner. I saw something special in Marcus Davis the very first time I saw him play. His calm demeanor was that of a veteran hitter, and he had great bat control. The manager for the Emeralds, Robbie Wine, and I both agreed that he was easily one of the best hitters in the organization, so in spring training Robbie fought to get him on our team in Oregon. Davis was already a gifted athlete with a good foundation, but he was open to getting better. Robbie and I both wanted to see Marcus succeed because we thought he was being overlooked by the organization. Many scouts sang his praises and were impressed by the fact that he rarely got rattled at the plate. One scout even joked that "he had ice in his veins," and I agreed. I had many talks with him about pitch trajectory, location, and swing path, and he was a believer. We invested a lot of time with him, and the results spoke for themselves. I am so thankful to have had the opportunity to work with a manger like Robbie Wine who allowed me the freedom to teach what I thought was right for this group of young men. At the end of the season, Davis tied for the league lead in doubles (23) and was in outright first for slugging percentage (SLG) (.537) and on-base plus slugging (OPS) (.948). He also finished fifth in batting average (.322) and fourth in on-base percentage (OBP) (.411). Davis' success was a direct result of his ability to execute the game plan we constructed. We were proud of the improvements Marcus Davis made to his game and that he was able to take it to the next level.

Trea Turner was touted as a defensive wizard and base stealer. But, in my assessment, he was a complete baseball player with all the skills necessary to make it to the majors. Turner was supposed to be with the Emeralds for only a week and then be moved up to middle-A, but he got off to a slow start offensively. Trea was a first-round pick (big money kid), so I didn't want to mess with him a whole lot. I figured I'd flip him a few balls and let him be on his way. I gave a presentation to the team on my hitting philosophy, and Trea was all ears. I could tell that after almost three weeks of struggling that his interest was piqued, so we talked after the presentation and he asked lots of questions. I asked if I could show him some data on pitch location and swing path, and we collaborated on what adjustments he would be comfortable making. I assured him that with everything he was doing right, he needed only to make a slight adjustment in his load to start seeing improvement. That night Trea got three hits. That same night, he got called up to Fort Wayne to help with some of their defensive issues, but he took a little offensive help with him as well. Before he left I asked him not to say anything to anyone about what we had discussed because the organization had its own philosophy and I didn't want to step on any toes—but at the same time—I knew I couldn't sit back and watch him continue to struggle when I knew that I could help. He went on to hit .369 in middle-A Fort Wayne and went 5-5 in a single game in the Arizona Fall League later that year. I continued to follow Trea's video online, and he continued to do everything we had discussed. I saw an interview with him and he said all he was focusing on was one of the key things we had worked on together.

I am well aware of the English proverb, "success has many fathers, but failure is an orphan." From day one I made these young men aware that they were too talented to not be having more success. I did not change their athletic ability. These were all very talented ball players before they ever met me. But regardless of the talent, if you don't have volumes of success, your talent means nothing. I simply gave them a game plan at the plate. I showed them where the largest volumes of pitches settle and helped with their mechanics and swing path, and they put in the work. It was a total collaborative effort. The fact that they were all intelligent enough to process the information and mentally strong enough to stand in the batter's box and execute what they'd learned, says a lot about these young men.

Chapter 9

The Shift

I can't talk about hitting without discussing the "shift." The infield shift in baseball is the drastic realignment of the infielders from their normal positions to blanket a particular side of the ball field. Mostly used against left-handed batters, it's designed to defend against extra-base hits pulled hard into the gaps between the first and second base side of the field.

As a former player myself, I can't believe that players continue to hit into the shift. A hitter that continues to hit into the shift is essentially doing the same thing over and over again and expecting a different result. And we know this is pure insanity. This is a prime example of your average pull hitter Again, I'll repeat, you are not just a self-proclaimed pull hitter (or you shouldn't be anyway). What this tells me is that hitters that perpetually hit into the shift don't understand the downward trajectory of all pitches. Nor do they understand the swing path needed to accommodate those pitches to get the ball up and over the infield to beat the shift.

A pull hitter MUST adjust his swing path, or he will continue to struggle. As discussed earlier in the Jon Roegele study, with the strike zone dropping, it becomes even more difficult for a pull hitter to be successful because he will continue to swing right over pitches. It is not about what you like to do as a hitter. If a hitter truly understood his value to himself and to the team, he would make it more of a priority to become an opposite field hitter.

The only real benefit to being a pull hitter is a handful of additional home runs. But look at all of the hit and extra-base hit production that a pull hitter leaves on the table by not adjusting his swing to the shift. Pull hitters feel that they hit for more power when they pull the ball. I would like for them to understand that if they learn the swing mechanics detailed in this book, not only will they still hit for power, they will also hit for extra-base hits and ultimately defeat the shift. At the end of the day a hitter should want to improve his numbers not just for himself but for the team as a whole, since this extra hit production is needed to make the postseason.

Here's the best example I can give to break it down even further. I was recently watching an episode of *ESPN First Take* with Stephen A. Smith. He mentioned a conversation where Donald Trump was giving him a piece of advice. Donald said, "Stephen A., let me tell you something, and don't you ever forget it. If you go to the bank and borrow $3 million and you can't pay it back, then YOU have a problem. But if you go to the bank and borrow $300 million and can't pay it back, then WE have a problem!" Meaning that a lot more people are going to get involved and be affected when there's more money in jeopardy. The same goes when we're speaking of the shift. If we're talking about a couple of rookies making league minimum going out and continuously hitting into the shift, then that's just something they need to go down to the minor leagues and work on. But when we start talking about a heavy hitter who's making $10-20 million a year and draining a team's payroll, then the whole team has a problem if they can't get him to make an adjustment in his swing to beat the shift. It becomes a problem for the organization as a whole, not just the player.

Part IV

The Team Approach

Chapter 10

Teams Need Consistent Run Production to Make the Postseason

So why does pitch location and swing path matter to a team on a collective basis? How could it possibly impact how teams are constructed or make trades? The answer may sound overly simple, but in the current world of number crunching and complicated algorithms, sometimes the simplest answer is the best one. In order to have the best chance of making the postseason, over the course of an entire season, teams need to average scoring more runs than they allow per game. It may sound overly simplistic, but to achieve it, is not easy. Teams that get nine hits per game, score five runs, and allow no more than four runs can consider themselves among the elite teams with a strong chance of making the postseason. Below are the regular season averages of all teams in the American League that made the postseason from 1973 to 2013:[22]

Average number of hits per game (HPG): 9.33

- Lowest qualifying HPG: 8.12 (OAK 1974, 2012)
- Highest qualifying HPG: 10.34 (CLE 1996)

Average number of walks per game (BBG): 3.61

- Lowest qualifying BBG: 2.47 (KC 1984)
- Highest qualifying BBG: 4.78 (SEA 2000)

Average number of runs per game (RPG): 5.05

- Lowest qualifying RPG: 4.07 (BAL 1974)
- Highest qualifying RPG: 6.23 (CLE 1999)

---

22 Compiled data is from www.mlb.com.

Average number of runs allowed per game (RAG): 4.3

- Lowest qualifying RAG: 3.40 (OAK 1974)[23]
- Highest qualifying RAG: 5.54 (BAL 1996)

Average difference between runs scored and runs allowed per game (RPG-RAG): +.75

- Lowest qualifying RPG-RAG: -.08 (KC 1981 (SS) and 1984)
- Highest qualifying RPG-RAG: 1.91 (NYY 1998)

In the past 40 years, only two American League teams have made the post-season with negative RPG-RAG: the 1987 Minnesota Twins (-.012) and the 1984 Kansas City Royals (-.08).[24] At the end of the 2014 season, the five American League teams that qualified for the playoffs recorded the following data points:

Team	RPG	HPG	BBG	RAG	RPG-RAG
Baltimore	4.35	8.85	2.47	3.66	+0.69
Detroit	4.67	9.61	2.73	4.35	+0.32
Los Angeles	4.77	9.03	3.03	3.88	+0.89
Kansas City[25]	*4.02*	*10.25*	*2.34*	*3.85*	*+0.17*
Oakland	4.50	8.35	3.67	3.53	+0.97

Some interesting things jump out from this data. First, the Orioles averaged 4.35 runs per game while getting 8.85 hits per game, while the Royals averaged 4.02 runs per game averaging 10.25 hits per game. That would indicate that the Royals had a lot of singles and had to manufacture runs with speed through steals and bunts rather than through extra-base hits. In fact, the Royals were 13th out of 15 in the American league with 1456 base hits, including last in home runs with 95. However they were 1st in stolen bases and 4th in doubles and 5th in triples. It is interesting to note that the 2014 American League leaders in extra-base hits were Detroit, Baltimore and the LA Angels, in that order, each of the three division winners. This is more proof that you need to get the ball in the air for extra-base hits.

Below is the RPG-RAG of the three teams from each division that finished

---

23 The New York Yankees averaged allowing 3.21 runs per game through 107 games of the strike shortened 1981 season.
24 The Kansas City Royals also qualified for the playoffs in 1981's strike-shortened season with a RPG-RAG of -.08 through 103 games.
25 In 2014, the Kansas City Royals ultimately won the American League pennant.

in second place in their division or did not make one of the two wild card spots. Each team was below the historic average of +.75 and below the RPG-RAG of the first place team in their division. Of these three teams, only Seattle seriously contended for one of the two wild card spots during the last week of the season but its differential between runs per game (RPG) and runs against (RAG) was less than the two teams from its division that qualified for the playoffs.

- New York Yankees: -1.00 (3.09 – 4.09)
- Cleveland: +0.10 (4.13 – 4.03)
- Seattle: +0.49 (3.91 – 3.42)

In no way am I suggesting that a team that scores five runs will win every game they play. To the contrary, there will be plenty of times that five runs in a game will not be enough to win. And sometimes only one run will be needed to win. That's baseball. But I am suggesting a daily goal to achieve and exceed. A team that consistently scores at least **five** runs a game will have a very high likelihood of winning a significant majority of their games. Put another way, a team that cannot score five runs on average over the course of the season will have a hard time (although not impossible) of reaching the postseason.

In order to score five runs a game, a team needs to get a lot of hits: almost nine or ten per game (in addition to three walks). That's a lot of offense. Simple math implies that teams should be able to score one run for every two hits. We all know that two consecutive singles usually do not manufacture a run. And, sometimes, even three consecutive singles do not score a run. So teams need to be efficient with their hits and run production. Indeed, there are lots of combinations (depending upon the number of outs) to score one run on two hits or less:

- BB + stolen base + single/extra-base hit (XBH)[26]
- BB + SAC + single/XBH
- Single + stolen base + single/XBH
- Single + BB + single/XBH
- Single + SAC + single/XBH
- Double + single/XBH

---

26 I use "single/XBH" because, with a runner in scoring position, a single does not always result in a run being scored. Hard line drives and ground balls may require the runner to stop at third. But an extra-base hit will almost always result in the runner scoring from second base.

- Double + SAC[27] + single/XBH

- Double + SAC + SAC

- Triple + single/XBH

- Triple + SAC

- Home Run

Let's take this even a step further and talk a little bit about how individual players can get a team to the postseason. When young elite players like Derek Jeter, Albert Pujols and Todd Helton came on the scene and started getting 200 hits, it's no wonder their respective teams started making the postseason. When one player has the production of almost one and a half players, it is a great benefit to a team. It's no secret that all of the players mentioned are excellent "low in the zone" hitters. And that's not the only value in having these kinds of special players on a team. Most importantly, their production is such that it saves teams money in the long run by allowing them not to have to take on another salary. And this leads us right into payroll.

---

27 In the definition of a SAC, when a runner is on second with no outs, I would include groundout to the right side. However, ground balls are not optimal and a proper swing path with an uptick would not result in a ground ball.

Chapter 11

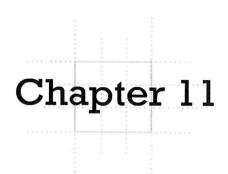

How Hitting Low in the Zone Affects Payroll

As you can imagine once I found all of the extra hit production, it became the perfect storm and a natural progression for the discussion to lead into how hitting low in the zone could affect payroll. More importantly, how it could help teams decrease their payrolls. I know that one of the ideas behind *Moneyball* initially was to build teams by acquiring players with undervalued attributes (e.g. on-base percentage (OBP) and slugging percentage), at a cheaper cost and still be competitive. Present-day *Moneyball* has evolved with much more complex measures of productivity, and it will continue to evolve as teams search to find advantages. I can anticipate that people who swear by the numbers will try to dismiss the idea that hitting low in the zone can positively impact the relationship between lower payrolls and greater production. So be it. But I truly believe that teaching players to hit low in the zone will do just that. Why? Because teams that rely on walks and home runs as a measure of productivity are unlikely to be successful in the long run against pitchers with excellent control and above average stuff (i.e. the pitchers most likely faced in the postseason). Sound hitting mechanics give teams multiple ways to win games. In turn, teams can get as much production from a player with a lower salary as a player with a higher one. Then again, this is just my unscientific opinion. But my experience as a major league player tells me that I'm right.

To further confirm this, let's look at the 2013 Cardinals as an example. Continuing under the assumption that 1,500 hits will get a team to the postseason, the Cards had a team total of 1494 hits. Out of that 1494, 952 cost them $8.8 million

(40 additional hits came from the pitching staff). So roughly 1,000 of their total hits came from this budget. Their three highest paid players, (Carlos Beltran, Yadier Molina and Matt Holliday) put together a total of 481 hits at a cost of $44 million combined. Not to downplay these players because they've been good for a very long time, but remember the focus here is to find production at a cheaper cost, right? You only have two options, hits or walks. In this case, it's not walks. I'm not saying that replacing these three players will be easy, but you can get three average everyday rookies that'll give you at least 120 hits each per season. Realistically we're only trying to find an additional 40 hits per player. The additional 120 hits can be found easily by teaching players to hit low in the zone.

Also noteworthy from the 2013 Cardinals is that Matt Carpenter had 199 of the team's 1,494 hits with a salary of only a little over half a million dollars. Out of his almost 200 hits, 147 were 2.5 feet and lower, again major success low in the zone.[28] So this tells us that you don't need a superstar player that's only going to produce 150-160 hits per season with a $10 million price tag. You just need to position your reasonably priced players to make adjustments low in the zone, and you're well on your way to the postseason with money to spare!

Let's put this into everyday terms. I have a friend who works for a company that generated $720 million in 2014. Out of that $720 million, $23 million was profit. And they worked their backsides off for that. They have over 7,000 employees and thousands of customers. In baseball we have ball players with subpar production making upwards of $20 million in a single season. Where does it end? Teams have got to find a way to start controlling payroll. Players' salaries are continuously increasing due to television revenues even though the production on the field is decreasing along with the number of fans in the seats. The only way to bring fans back to the ballpark is through exciting baseball. Throughout history the game of baseball has always been remembered for offensive production. Babe Ruth began his career as a left-handed pitcher but is best remembered by his **power hitting**. Joe DiMaggio, Ted Williams, and Lou Brock all personified what fans came to the ballpark to see: doubles, home runs, and stolen bases. This exciting style of baseball is what puts butts in the seats—not walks and pitching.

What the data has shown time and time again is that teams whose identity is pitching either don't make it to the playoffs or have early exits. A high- pow-

---

28 Via www.brooksbaseball.net

ered offense, along with slightly above average pitching, will do more to get you through the playoffs than relying on pitching alone. Every time I see a pitcher get a $100 million contract I cringe. It is extremely difficult to win in the postseason with pitching alone. Teams must produce runs, and to do this hitters **must** entertain the lower part of the hitting zone. Here are some numbers from 2014 that really hit home:

Team	Payroll	Runs Against	Total Hits	Hits 2.5 ft & below
Padres	$90M	577	1199	741
Giants	$150M	614	1407	864
Dodgers	$235M	617	1476	888

Source: MLB.com and BrooksBaseball.net

What the data tells us is that San Diego gave up the least amount of runs in their division (577) which means that they pitched well enough to make it to the postseason. But according to the data, they needed to improve their offensive production. If we take a look at their division rivals, the Giants and the Dodgers, we see that both teams outperformed the Padres in total hits with 1,407 and 1,476 respectively as well as hit production low in the zone (2.5ft and below). The fact is the Padres were just not going to get another 200-300 hits over the heart of the plate in order to catch up with the offensive production of the Giants and Dodgers. Their $90 million payroll could have been just as competitive as their opponents if they had been more productive hitting low in the zone.

Now, let's shed a little light on how hitting low in the zone can help a team decrease its pitching payroll. No pitcher makes a living over the heart of the plate. It's no secret that pitchers believe their safe haven is down in the zone. But if what I am proposing is true, and teams can build swing mechanics to combat low pitches, it severely limits the options for pitchers while bringing their value down at the same time. They will no longer be able to make a living throwing low in the zone. Teams would then be able to spend their money on offense and less on pitching. And I've already discussed how you can control your offensive payroll by consistently producing hitters who are proficient low in the zone. The name of the game then becomes **outscoring** the opposing team, not **outpitching** them.

Hitting Low in the Zone: A New Baseball Paradigm

Another little something to think about...

Most teams spend way too much money on pitching. The point that seems to be clear is that there's no pitching goal that can be obtained that will overcome a weak offense over the course of a season. Baseball people get so caught up in wanting to take sides where hitting and pitching are concerned, or they feel that there should be a balance between the two when this is not the case. The fact remains that even a perfect game cannot be won without some kind of offensive help and a whole lot of defense for that matter. Unfortunately, we cannot quantify defense, but as far as pitching is concerned, there still needs to be one more run scored than given up to win a game. Let's use the magical 1998 Yankees World Series championship season for this example. We had both phenomenal pitching and a high-powered offense that year. And when I say high-powered, that's putting it mildly. The perception was that the pitching was just as impactful as the offense. But when you take a closer look at the numbers, it's debatable. When the pitching staff gives up four runs per game on average (which was the case that season), but the offense scores six runs per game on average, and you end up with the win no one really cares who the hero is.[29] It was unreal how many come-from-behind victories we had that year due to the explosive offense. A high-powered offense can hide a multitude of sins on the mound or at least make a pitcher's less-than-perfect performance a mere memory. Again, if teams want to get the best bang for their buck, it just makes sense to put more money towards a low-ball hitting offense than a pitcher who needs both offensive and defensive reinforcement to get the job done.

---

29 Via Baseball reference.com, in 162 games the 1998 Yankees scored 965 runs for a 5.94 average runs scored per game and gave up 656 runs for a 4.04 average runs against per game.

Chapter 12

Do Teams Put Too Much Emphasis on Walks?

I can't talk about hitting without discussing walks. There's only two ways to get on base—to hit or to walk. Ever since *Moneyball,* hitting has become more and more confusing for players. They don't know whether to be swinging the bat or taking pitches. I know from my own experience as a player. After hitting .320 in 1999 with the Blue Jays, I had been advised to take more pitches to increase my on-base percentage (OBP) in 2000. By trying to take more pitches, I struggled. One of the downfalls of focusing on trying to walk is that it takes some of the aggressive edge away from a hitter. As a hitter you find yourself taking that first pitch which oftentimes ends up being a strike. This is beneficial to the pitcher. Any pitching coach will tell you that the best pitch in baseball is strike one. If a pitcher can get ahead of a hitter right out of the box, it increases his chances of getting him out. But at the same time, for a batter, it's hard to draw a walk unless you take the first pitch. In my case back in 2000, it was obvious that I was trying to draw more walks even to the media. So obvious that I would be watching *Baseball Tonight* on television and would hear Harold Reynolds screaming, "Homer swing the bat, and stop taking all of those pitches!" I made my mind up the following year that I was going back to the aggressive style of hitting that had earned me that .300 average in the past. If walks came, fine. If not, that was fine too. Going back to my tried-and-true style helped me finish up 2001 batting .306.

Over the years, the need to draw more walks has done more harm to the game of baseball than good. Excessive walking has slowed down the pace of games, led to lower run production and caused an overall lack of aggressiveness at the plate. When I was coaching with the Padres minor league system in 2014,

Hitting Low in the Zone: A New Baseball Paradigm

they considered an eight pitch at-bat to be a quality at-bat. That's just ridiculous especially when it oftentimes ends in an out. How do we speed up the game? You either: a) put the pitcher on a clock or; b) speed up the batter. And how do you speed up the batter? It's not by forcing him to keep one foot in the batter's box. You do it by making him more aggressive at hittable pitches. Yadier Molina is a great example of a very productive and efficient hitter. In 2013, with 541 plate appearances he saw only 1,884 pitches. He took 883 of those pitches, swung at 1,001 and ended the season with 161 hits (44 doubles and 12 home runs), 80 RBI, and a .319 batting average.[30] And with all of that production, he still managed to finish with 30 walks. Molina is not just a free swinger. He's just more aggressive on hittable pitches, not necessarily strikes. There are countless other hitters who saw more than 2,500 pitches with substantially less production. If every batter saw 2,000 or less pitches, this would speed up the game a great deal. Hitting low in the zone with the proper mechanics allows hitters to see and capitalize on more hittable pitches which not only speeds up the game but helps a team to get that offensive production that's missing.

Walks are important, but they are not a substitute for hits. Walks should be supplementary to hits. When hitting low in the zone, walks should occur more naturally. A disciplined hitter looking for low pitches will draw walks without sacrificing his aggressiveness. A team will not be successful if it relies on walks as its primary means to get men on base or drive in runs. But a walk can result in a runner in scoring position if the walked batter has speed and steals second base. If not, it will take at least two singles or potentially an extra-base hit to score the runner from first base. And a ground ball usually means a double play. Sabermetricians don't get scared! I believe that there is great value in players who simply get on base, but those players need bats behind them that can drive them in!

Singles alone don't do the job either. Two singles don't necessarily result in a run. A team could have six or seven hits in a game—all singles—and score no runs. Indeed, a team could get three hits in an inning and still not score a run. Singles are generally two-thirds of a team's total hits. But it is what happens after the single or walk that makes the difference between scoring and leaving men on base. I have a funny story that I'll never forget to prove this point. In 1998 when I played with the Yankees, they would put me in to pinch run because I was known for stealing bases and igniting a spark in the lineup. Joe Torre put me in

---

30 Baseball Info Solutions, *The Bill James Handbook 2014,* (Chicago, Illinois: ACTA Sports, 2013), 198, 358.

during the ninth inning to pinch run for Chili Davis who had just doubled. The next hit was a one-hop line drive single to center field, so I had to stay on second or risk being doubled off. The following hit was a line drive to left field, but I was able to advance to third base. It took a **third** single to score me (see the following box scores for the play-by-play)[31]. When I got back to the dugout, Joe Torre said, "Heck, Bushy, I could have left Chili out there for that!" It still bothered Joe some years after, because every now and then when I'd see him at an event, he'd remind me of this very game and we'd laugh about it. This just goes to show the importance of having a swing path that gets the ball in the air for extra-bases and aids in moving the runner over more efficiently. It's just too much work to hit three singles and only score one run from second base.

Top of the 9th, Yankees Batting, Ahead 8-5, Orioles' Alan Mills facing 5-6-7					
Inning	Score	Outs	At Bat	Batter	Pitcher	Play Description
t9	8-5	0	NYY	C. Davis	A. Mills	Double to LF (Line Drive); Sojo to 3B
						Homer Bush pinch runs for Chili Davis (DH) batting 6th
t9	8-5	0	NYY	R. Ledee	A. Mills	Single to CF (Line Drive); Sojo scores; Bush stays at 2B
t9	9-5	0	NYY	J. Posada	A. Mills	Single to LF (Line Drive); Bush to 3B; Ledee to 2B
t9						Jesse Orosco replaces A. Mills (pitching)
t9	9-5	0	NYY	S. Brosius	J. Orosco	Single to RF (Ground Ball thru 2B-1B); **Bush Scores**; Ledee to 3B; Posada to 2B

Let's touch on how too many walks can work against a team. In 2013, the Cincinnati Reds drew 585 walks. Out of the 585, almost 250 came from two of their best hitters, Joey Votto and Shin-Soo Choo. This affected their ability to drive in runs because their main focus was on drawing walks. When two out of three of a team's best hitters are walking excessively instead of driving in runs, the walks tend to lose value over the course of the season which ultimately hurts the team as a whole. Reds former manager Dusty Baker has said in the past that, "clogging up the bases isn't that great to me." He goes on to say that, "OBP means nothing if it's not followed by RBI." Votto and Choo were left on the bases quite a bit that year. Baker said, "You can get on the base all you want to but if you don't have guys driving you in, it doesn't matter." He continues with, "It's not called walking, it's called hitting," as he voiced his frustration with the two players' ability to get on base but inability to score more runs.[32] So what good does walking do if you can't capitalize by driving in the runs?

Economics principle, the "law of diminishing returns" or "diminishing marginal productivity" states that "if one input in the production of a commodity is

---

31 http://www.baseball-reference.com/boxes/BAL/BAL199809180.shtml
32 Anthony Castrovince, "Votto and Choo are down with OBP," *MLB.com*, May 30, 2013, http://m.mlb.com/news/article/49061878/anthony-castrovince-joey-votto-and-shin-soo-choo-are-down-with-obp.

increased while all other inputs are held fixed, a point will eventually be reached at which additions of the input yield progressively smaller, or diminishing increases in output".[33] I am no economist, but I think this principle applies to teams that rely too heavily on walks as a substitute for hits. At some point, walks are no longer useful, and hits are needed to drive in the walks. Put another way, perhaps more simply, too many walks can hurt a team's ability to score runs and win championships. Possibly one of the best examples of walking too much is the outlier Oakland A's. I mentioned before how in my research they stood out amongst all of the teams. Over the last decade the very thing that the A's have been best known for has become their Achilles heel. Again, in 2014 Oakland was first in walks with 586, 22nd in hits with 1,354 and fourth in runs scored with 729 but only squeaked into the playoffs with a wild card spot. Why is this? They seemed to be doing everything right. With their increased on-base percentage from the accumulation of walks, effective pitching low in the zone, and their ability to elevate the ball into the air, one would think they'd make it further in the postseason. The excessive walking is hurting them. It's the very thing keeping them from winning a championship. If the A's could have turned 80-100 of those walks into hits, they would have been unstoppable. They would have been the only team to score over 800 runs that season which was very plausible if they could have gotten their hitters to be even more aggressive on hittable pitches. Hits are always more productive than walks.

The following data from 2014 tells a story. Teams need to caution against too much reliance on walks as a substitute for hits. A large amount of walks does not necessarily translate to wins or success. The teams in bold print all made the playoffs. Take a look at their walks and hits ranking. Plenty of them did not rely on walks. If they were high in the walks category and made the postseason, they were also high in hits or had sufficient enough pitching to keep runs against down. The Royals were 30th in walks (380) but were the American League champs that lasted to game seven of the World Series. The A's were first in walks (586) but got knocked out early.

---

[33] Encyclopedia Britannica Online. Encyclopedia Britannica Inc., 2014. Web. 10 Nov. 2014
http://www.britannica.com/EBchecked/topic/163723/diminishing-returns.

Hitting Low in the Zone: A New Baseball Paradigm

Team	Payroll Rank	Walks Rank	Hits Rank	Runs Rank	Wins Rank
Dodgers+	**1st ($235.2m)**	**6th (519)**	**3rd (1476)**	**6th (718)**	**4th (94)**
Yankees	2nd ($203.8m)	17th (452)	23rd (1349)		
Phillies	3rd ($180.0m)	18th (443)	20th (1356)		
Red Sox	4th ($162.8m)	3rd (535)	21st (1355)		
Tigers+	**5th ($162.2m)**	**18th (443)**	**1st (1557)**	**2nd (757)**	**5th (90)**
Angels+	**6th ($155.6m)**	**13th (492)**	**4th (1464)**	**1st (773)**	**1st (98)**
*Giants***	*7th ($154.1m)*	*21st (427)*	*11th (1407)*	*12th (665)*	*8th (88)*
Rangers	8th ($136.0m)	23rd (417)	13th (1400)	17th (637)	
Nationals+	**9th ($134.7m)**	**7th (517)**	**12th (1403)**	**9th (686)**	**2nd (96)**
Blue Jays	10th ($132.6m)	10th (502)	7th (1435)	5th (723)	
Diamondbacks	11th ($112.6m)	27th (398)	16th (1379)		
Reds	12th ($112.3m)	25th (415)	29th 1282		
Cardinals^	**13th ($111.0m)**	**15th (471)**	**17th (1371)**	**23rd (619)**	**5th (90)**
Braves	14th ($110.0m)	14th (472)	26th (1316)		
Orioles^	**15th ($107.4m)**	**26th (401)**	**8th (1434)**	**8th (705)**	**2nd (96)**
Brewers	16th ($103.8m)	22nd (423)	18th (1366)	15th (650)	
Rockies	17th ($95.8m)	28th (397)	2nd (1551)	3rd (755)	
Mariners	18th ($92.08m)	29th (396)	24th (1328)		
Royals*	**19th ($92.0m)**	**30th (380)**	**5th (1456)**	**14th (651)**	**7th (89)**
White Sox	20th ($91.1m)	23rd (417)	13th (1400)	13th (660)	
Padres	21st ($90.0m)	16th (468)	30th (1199)		
Mets	22nd ($89.05m)	8th (516)	28th (1306)		
Cubs	23rd ($89.0m)	20th (442)	27th (1315)		
Twins	24th ($85.7m)	2nd (544)	9th (1412)	7th (715)	
A's++	**25th ($83.4m)**	**1st (586)**	**22nd (1354)**	**4th (729)**	**8th (88)**
Indians	26th ($82.5)	9th (504)	10th (1411)	11th (669)	
Pirates++	**27th ($78.1m)**	**5th (520)**	**6th (1436)**	**10th (682)**	**8th (88)**
Rays	28th ($77.0m)	4th (527)	19th (1361)		
Marlins	29th ($47.5m)	11th (501)	15th (1399)	16th (645)	
Astros	30th ($44.5m)	12th (495)	25th (1317)		

+ Eliminated in Division Series
** World Series Champion
^ Eliminated in Championship Series
* American League Champion
++ Eliminated in Wild Card

Again, it is important to not rely on walks as a replacement for hits. The key is a balance between walks and hits. To make the most compelling argument, let's go back to 2013. The Cincinnati Reds had 178 more **walks** than the Milwaukee Brewers but scored only **50** more runs. The Detroit Tigers had 178 more **hits** than the Los Angeles Dodgers that produced **149** more runs—more hits are better than walks for sure.[34] Not to mention, all of the 178 extra hits the Tigers had were 2.5 feet down to the ground.[35] If a team can find more hits, that would be a better and easier option to run production than trying to draw more walks. There's no magic number of walks to predict making it to the postseason. But 1,500 hits will get you there, **IF** you can control the number of runs scored against. There are pitches and hits low in the zone if you have the right approach and swing path.

Let me make a generalization here: Baseball fans come to the park to see home runs, doubles and exciting play—they don't come to see walks. Knowledgeable fans know the importance of walks, but it is not why they pay good money to see games. As a form of entertainment, we have a responsibility to give the fans what they want. What they want is a world championship and exciting baseball. Walks, while an important piece to achieving those goals, should not be the primary focus.

---

34 See http://mlb.mlb.com/stats/sortable
35 Via www.brooksbaseball.net

Chapter 13

How Statistics Can Make or Break a Team

Modern baseball is a game dominated by statistics and so-called "sabermetrics." Sabermetricians have become invaluable to nearly every team's front office for assessments of player values in connection with drafting and trades. I understand the need to find any edge possible and for teams to find hidden values in players that will make their teams better overall. I was a casualty of sabermetrics when it was introduced into the Toronto Blue Jays organization in 2002. In the book *Moneyball*, there is a long narrative about when the Blue Jays were sold to Rogers Communications at the end of the 2000 season and appointed Paul Godfrey as the team's CEO. Mr. Godfrey was "a man with no baseball experience [and] set out to run the business along rational lines." [36] Later in 2001, the Blue Jays hired the A's director of player development, J.P. Ricciardi. Mr. Godfrey is quoted as saying,

> *Of all the people I'd talked to, J.P. was the only one with a business plan and the only one who told me "You are spending too much money." He basically went through the lineup and said, "These people are all replaceable by people you've never heard of." And I said, "You sure?" And he said, "Look, if you can stand the heat in the media, I can make you cheaper and better. It'll take a couple of months to make you cheaper and a couple of years to make you better. But you'll be a lot better."* [37]

Immediately after he was hired, J.P. Ricciardi sought to recreate the success that Billy Beane had in Oakland and began by firing nearly all of the Blue Jays

---

[36] Michael Lewis, *Moneyball*, (New York: W.W. Norton & Company, 2004), 276.
[37] Ibid, 277.

scouts and got rid of "just about every highly paid, established big league player and replaced them with minor leaguers no one had ever heard of."

I was one of those "highly paid," "established" big leaguers that was replaced with minor leaguers. By May 2002, after three years with the Blue Jays, I was released as part of the Blue Jays need for a smaller payroll. I understand that baseball is a business and that your spot on the field is not guaranteed. I even understand that my statistics that mattered to sabermetricians combined with my salary level at that time didn't keep my place on the roster. It is the game.

What saddens me the most about the whole thing is **not** how it impacted my life—like I said—that's the business. What saddens me is that J.P.'s strategy negatively impacted the great fans of Toronto, dozens of players, staff and their families and has been an epic failure by virtually any yardstick. Did J.P. fulfill his promise to the Blue Jays when he said, *"It'll take a couple of months to make you cheaper and a couple of years to make you better?* **But you'll be a lot better.**" Let's look at the facts.

In 2001, the year before J.P. was hired the Blue Jays had a payroll of $76.8 million and had a record of 80 wins and 82 losses. They finished third in the American League East that year. The next year, J.P.'s first year as General Manager, they had the same payroll but wound up with two less wins and a record of 78 and 84. They again finished third.

Between 2003 and 2005 when J.P. really saw the benefits of a smaller payroll ($51.2 m, $50 m, $47.5 m), their production remained virtually unchanged with 86 wins in 2003, 67 wins in 2004 and 80 wins in 2005.[38] Again, the Blue Jays never finished higher than third in any of those years.

Now, one could say, "Wait a minute Homer, J.P. was able to produce the same number of wins in those three years with about 1/3 less money. Isn't that a real benefit?" But baseball is not won on the balance sheet. During J.P.'s eight year tenure in Toronto, the Blue Jays did not make the postseason and in his final year had a larger payroll and fewer wins than when he took over. In fact, as is evident from the following chart, during J.P.'s years at the helm, the reverse effect of *Moneyball* occurred. As the Blue Jays' payroll went down, they managed fewer wins. And when its payroll went up, it bought more wins. Take a look at the next chart:

---

38 All Toronto Blue Jays payroll and wins data via https://www.baseballprospectus.com/compensation/cots/al-east/toronto-blue-jays/ and http://www.baseball-reference.com/teams/TOR/

Hitting Low in the Zone: A New Baseball Paradigm

The vertical axis represents dollars (in millions).

The horizontal axis represents the years with 1=2002 and 8=2009.

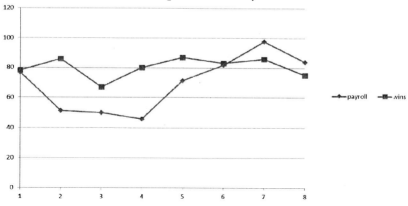

In fact, when you put it in absolute terms, the Blue Jays were worse off after J.P.'s years at the helm. The Blue Jays average cost per win in 2002 was just under $1 million ($985,440 per win) and in J.P.'s last year as general manager (2009), the average cost per win was over $1.1 million ($1,119,526 per win) with no postseason appearances to show for it. So at the end of his tenure, the Blue Jays weren't run cheaper and they weren't a lot better. By that measure, J.P. Ricciardi failed and many suffered the consequences for it. What I think J.P. (and others like him) fail to understand is that walks, on-base percentage and slugging percentage don't win games by themselves. What is needed is a team approach that scores a lot of runs, which translates into wins.

As I've said, I understand the need to find any edge possible and for teams to find hidden values in players that will make their teams better overall. Sabermetrics is but one tool that can help organizations and individuals. If I had one critique of sabermetrics, it would be that it uses a player's value yesterday as a predictor of his value tomorrow. This does not account for an individual's internal will, his motivation to become better at what he does and the measure of success the team achieves when the individual puts his personal goals subordinate to the team. In a sense, sabermetrics "plays the odds" when it comes to player values and assumes no improvement and that no individual can do something spectacular.

Noreena Hertz, author of "*Eyes Wide Open: How to Make Smart Decisions in a Confusing World*," made a similar commentary in the Wall Street Journal on October 22, 2014, about trying to quantify the unquantifiable. She stated:

> *In the "Age of The Cult of the Measurable," our challenge is to seek out actively and pay attention to information that cannot yet be quantified is important.... Yet thinking about different potential scenarios, and how they might play out, and developing a host of contingency plans is essential behavior... Then there's of course the problem with models in general: future sales projections; future cash flow etc. etc. These assume a linear trajectory and a world that is relatively static. But in a world as fast moving and complex as ours such assumptions more often than not will not hold. By devaluing that which cannot be measured, by assuming that history inevitable is on a forward march, we risk not only making poorer decision but also distorting our priorities and goals.* [39]

As it relates to baseball, John Sexton said it beautifully in his book, *Baseball as a Road to God: Seeing Beyond the Game,* with the following passage:

> *There is wonder in the vast variety of numbers that baseball produces. And it is undeniable that sabermetrics provide valuable tools to the front office and fan alike; evidence of all kinds is critical to making good decisions—the more, the better.*
>
> *But the most important elements of baseball cannot be measured. Some of them simply are immeasurable.* **And the numbers can miss the essence of the matter; the facts can become false idols, obscuring truth in horrible reductionism.** *Simply scribbling F7 on a scorecard after a spectacular catch in left field doesn't capture the magic of the moment or the actual talent involved—just as musical notes on a sheet of paper cannot capture the beautiful sounds of a violin.* [40]

Being reduced to a sabermetric statistic at the end of the 2002 season was ironic for me personally. I had spent my entire life avoiding being a statistic. To view my youth and chances of success, an outsider could fall into what John Sexton cautioned about, that "... *the numbers can miss the essence of the matter; the facts can become false idols, obscuring truth in horrible reductionism.*" My life did not progress on a "linear trajectory." If a sabermetrics model was used on me in the 1980s to

---

39 Noreena Hertz, "What Companies Lose By Obsessing Over Metrics," *Wall Street Journal. Com* (blog), October 22, 2014, (6:41 a.m.), http://blogs.wsj.com/experts/2014/10/22/what-companies-lose-by-obsessing-over-metrics.
40 Sexton, John, "*Baseball as a Road to God: Seeing Beyond the Game*" (2013) pp 64-65.

predict my "value" in the future, the result would not reflect where I am today and what I have achieved. I have always refused to be reduced to a statistic. And this is the philosophy I bring to hitting and all aspects of baseball. I reject the idea that a hitter who has historically been an underachiever is doomed to repeat it for the rest of his (possibly short without change) career.

Chapter 14

Conclusion

I've talked about a lot of things, but in the end what I'd like to make clear is that in order for a player to maximize his success at the plate, he has to get two-thirds of his production low in the hitting zone from the ground up to the top of the knees. The one thing I learned from corporate America is that you make a billion-dollar company's bottom line better through consistent production. In baseball, that production is runs which are a direct result of hits. And the only way, I mean the ONLY way to get consistent hits is to focus your attention where the largest volume of pitches settle and to have the proper mechanics to accommodate this area.

This is how it all came about for me and hitting low in the zone. I started to research why Mike Trout was so much better than everyone else while at the same time looking for an edge for my own son. I quickly found that it was largely due to the fact that he was a prolific low-ball hitter. Bingo! Further research led me to his swing path. I felt like Mike Trout's production could be reproduced over and over again. What would happen if a team could have five or six players (or unlimited) exactly like him? How would this affect payroll? How could this influence the way teams build rosters and make trades? How could this help increase the chances of teams making the postseason?

In order for a team to get the 1,500-1,600 hits necessary to make the postseason, the team's hitting approach has to be from the ground up NOT the top down within the hitting zone. To be even more specific, a team needs anywhere from 900-1,000 hits from the ground up to the knees depending on that team's division. Hitters must be more aggressive on hittable pitches, not just what they believe to be strikes. Many of the elite hitters of past and present (aware or not) already possess some of the mechanics I've detailed. Others need only to make a few minor adjustments to see huge payoffs in production. More players, teams, and organizations could benefit from having an open mind and the willingness to change their perspective on hitting thereby shifting the balance of power back to the batter's box. I feel confident saying to any young player looking to become a major league hitter—whether it is youth, high school or minor leagues—it's important for them to build their hitting mechanics and swing path to accommodate hitting low in the zone.

Many of the new players who were top prospects in the minor leagues—Kris Bryant (Cubs), Byron Buxton (Twins), and Gregory Polanco (Pirates)—just to name a few, all have the swing mechanics that are necessary for consistent success. Add some of the established elite hitters of today, Mike Trout, Andrew McCutchen, and Miguel Cabrera who are also masters of low-ball hitting—and this philosophy speaks for itself. Now that I've proven through data and common sense, the importance of my approach, I challenge you to study the video of some of the many hitters mentioned in this book and see for yourselves if you still believe what you've always believed to be true about hitting and its impact on the game of baseball.

My Afterhoughts and Hope for the Future of Baseball

Being an African American, I have a personal interest in combatting the steady decline of blacks at the major league level. I feel strongly that the hitting low in the zone philosophy can level the playing field and gives any player the ability to fulfill their dreams of becoming a major league player. Personally, I'd like to see an improvement in the process of drafting and developing young prospects from within our inner cities.

My hope is that my own son, as well as other black kids, will have the same opportunity to realize their dreams of playing in the major leagues if they work hard and stay on the right path. From a baseball perspective, never has it been more important to emphasize this point to our inner city youth than now because there are fewer black baseball players in the major leagues today than there were nearly 30 years ago. In 2014, only 8.3% of the players on opening day rosters identified themselves as African American or black. This is more than a 50% reduction from those that identified themselves that way in 1986 (19%).[41] This is in stark contrast to the growth of Latin American players, which comprised 26.9% of MLB rosters in 2014.[42] In the summer of 2014, we saw a team from Jackie Robinson West Little League in Chicago, Illinois advance to the finals of the Little League World Series. On this team, we saw talented 11-to-13 year olds from our inner city demonstrate that baseball from these areas can be played at a level good enough to represent our country. I hope we seize this opportunity and help create a bridge for these young men and many others like them in our country's inner cities to

---

41 Tyler Kepner, "*M.L.B. Report Highlights Sobering Number of Black Players,*" The New York Times, April 9, 2014.
42 Jens Manuel Krogstad, "*67 Years after Jackie Robinson Broke the Color Barrier, Major League Baseball Looks Very Different,*" The Pew Research Center, April 16, 2014.

further their development. Jerry Manuel, former White Sox manager who serves on MLB's on-field diversity task force noted that, "*Little League is not a problem. Kids love to play Little League from 5 to 12, and they've got a great program. It's from 12 to 15. It's getting them from Little League to high school baseball is where we lose them — to football, to the streets, to basketball, to everything.*"[43]

From my experience, it is not about young black kids being less talented or not being coached as well as their counterparts. It is that they don't have the same resources. Coming from the inner city myself, I experienced firsthand what it was like to not have the funds to play baseball once I got to a certain level. If it weren't for donations of time and money from family, friends and coaches, I would have never made it as far as I did. Today's select and travel baseball programs are a financial strain on even the wealthiest of families. Inner city kids, most of whom come from single income families and get by on government assistance just can't afford to pay. This is not unique to the inner cities across the U.S. As a matter of fact, the economics are even worse in many Latin American communities. But why is there such a disparity in the number of blacks in the game compared to Latin players? Let's start with the fact that all thirty MLB teams have multimillion dollar baseball academies in the Dominican Republic for "promising" prospects. These academies house, feed, equip and train young prospects with the help of former professional Latin American players. They are essentially building players. It comes down to three simple things: time, money, and commitment. If the inner cities had just a few of these luxuries, we could produce black players at the same rate. Don't get me wrong, I have no issue with Latin players. They are some of the most talented players in the game today, and I have played with and remain friends with many of them. I would just like to see the same opportunities given to African Americans and others in our inner cities who can't afford to play the game. I am concerned that without it, blacks will have no interest in pursuing careers in our national pastime.

The good news is that on January 25, 2015, baseball Commissioner Robert D. Manfred Jr. mentioned possible improvements by making baseball more accessible in urban areas in his letter to fans taking on the responsibility of the position . . .

---

43 Tyler Kepner, "*M.L.B. Report Highlights Sobering Number of Black Players,*" The New York Times, April 9, 2014.

Hitting Low in the Zone: A New Baseball Paradigm

Dear Fans:

On the night of August 14, 2014, I left a Baltimore hotel after being elected Commissioner of Baseball. As I began to reply to the overwhelming number of congratulatory messages coming in, it hit me that I'd just been entrusted to protect the integrity of our National Pastime and to set a course that allows this great game to continue to flourish - now and in the years to come. Needless to say, I was deeply honored by the trust the owners placed in me.

Today is my first day as Commissioner, and I am incredibly excited to get to work. I am grateful to Commissioner Selig for his expertise and friendship. His leadership set a direction that led to historic success.

The mission before us is clear: To honor the game's history while welcoming new people to our great sport - people who will one day pass their love of baseball down through the generations. That is what our parents and grandparents did for us, and it is what we are doing for our own children. Baseball is a game firmly rooted in childhood experiences, and its vitality and growth rely heavily on giving young people from all backgrounds the opportunity to play and watch baseball.

This notion that baseball is the game of children is central to my core goals as Commissioner. Maybe that is because my own Little League experience in upstate Rome, New York was such an important part of my childhood. I will never forget my intense dedication to that club and to my teammates - each of whom I can still name to this day - and being part of a perfect game.

My top priority is to bring more people into our game - at all levels and from all communities. Specifically, I plan to make the game more accessible to those in underserved areas, especially in the urban areas where fields and infrastructure are harder to find. Giving more kids the opportunity to play will inspire a new generation to fall in love with baseball just as we did when we were kids. Expanding Little League, RBI and other youth baseball programs will also help sustain a steady and wide talent pool from which our clubs can draw great players and create

Hitting Low in the Zone: A New Baseball Paradigm

lifelong fans.

As Commissioner, I will draw closer connections between youth baseball and MLB. I want to inspire children's interest in baseball and help parents and coaches foster that passion. In the coming years, MLB will work with college, high school, amateur and youth baseball programs to help grow our game and to ensure that the best players and talent have the opportunity to pursue their dreams. I call it "One Baseball" - a partnership between all professional and amateur groups involved in our game.

Our children can look at MLB today and find a wave of new stars worthy of emulating both on and off the field. Players like Andrew McCutchen, Buster Posey, Giancarlo Stanton and Mike Trout and aces Madison Bumgarner, Felix Hernandez and Clayton Kershaw have powerful stories to tell - and MLB will tell them across every platform. We will continue to internationalize our game and to celebrate the fact that we have the most diverse rosters in the world. Our mission is to build upon this recent success by creating opportunities for the next wave of baseball talent. We also must continue to nurture inclusive environments for all the contributors to our game and our loyal fans.

Another priority for me is to continue to modernize the game without interfering with its history and traditions. Last season's expanded instant replay improved the game's quality and addressed concerns shared by fans and players. We made a dramatic change without altering the game's fundamentals. I look forward to tapping into the power of technology to consider additional advancements that will continue to heighten the excitement of the game, improve the pace of play and attract more young people to the game.

The Major League Clubs have bestowed an extraordinary opportunity upon me. My pledge is to work every single day to honor their faith in me and your love of this game. [44]

I am a product of the inner city of East St. Louis, and in my eyes, this is a positive step in the right direction towards bringing renewed excitement about the game of baseball back to the inner cities and urban areas alike. My hope is

---

44 Robert D. Manfred Jr., "Commissioner Rob Manfred's Letter to Fans," *MLB.com*, January 25, 2015, http://m.mlb.com/news/article/107424384/new-mlb-commissioner-rob-manfreds-letter-to-fans.

that increasing the number of blacks in the game will not only lead to relatable role models for younger generations of MLB hopefuls, but also encourage black spectators to return to ballparks in growing numbers. I am optimistic that the growth of these urban youth programs will have the ability to increase the number of black major league players while at the same time acting as a catalyst to give blacks more opportunities to pursue careers in coaching, managing and front office positions that would not have been thought possible otherwise.